Pub and Teashop Drives in Kent

Rupert Matthews

S.B. Publications

First published in 2010 by S.B. Publications
14 Bishopstone Road, Seaford, East Sussex
Tel: 01323 893498   Email: sbpublications@tiscali.co.uk

ISBN 978-185770-3481

Designed and Typeset by EH Graphics, East Sussex (01273) 515527

Contents

Introduction

If there are two marvellous things about England that can be found nowhere else on Earth, they are pubs and tearooms. Both types of hostelry have their fans, but together they sum up so much about England that is special and unique.

Each drive in this book starts at a pub and ends at a tearoom. The drives have been designed so that you will be able to have a light lunch at the pub, then travel leisurely through the beautiful Kent countryside - stopping off at points along the way - and arrive at the teashop in time for a nice fresh cup of tea and a slice of cake around teatime. What more pleasant way could there be to spend an afternoon in Kent?

Of course, each drive could be completed back to front, taking morning coffee at the tearooms and finishing at the pub for lunch. And it is always possible that you might find the stopping-off points so full of interest that you take longer than expected. I have tried to estimate how long an average person might spend looking around a church, battlefield or beauty spot, but these are only my guesses. You should keep an eye on the time. If it is slipping away from you, try to head off for the teashop, or pub, and come back to enjoy the stopping point later.

These journeys are for you to enjoy, not to rush through. Each drive has been planned to take you through the finest scenery that links the various places to be visited. For the most part the routes will take you along lanes and B roads, though some A roads are included when these offer good views. Generally, take your time and do it your way.

This book contains detailed driving instructions for each route. However, it is as well to keep a road map to hand on your outings. Local councils are skilled at introducing sudden changes to road markings and signs. What has been a right turn for years may suddenly become a bend in the road to the right while what used to be the straight road continuing on has become a turning to the left. And mini-roundabouts can be installed almost without notice.

Several of the teashops listed in this book are not open seven days a week during the winter. They are generally open at weekends year round, but if you are planning to complete one of these drives during the winter months, it would be wise to phone in advance. The pubs, by contrast, are generally open seven days a week all year round.

The author enjoys a cream tea at the Sandhurst Tea Rooms in Sandhurst.

6

The main doorway to Minster Abbey shows a limited amount of formal carving of the Norman period, giving no hint of the beauties within.

Isle of Thanet

Start: The Bell Inn, 2 High Street, Minster, Ramsgate, Kent CT12 4BU. Tel: 01843 821274

Finish: Victoria's Tea Room, 11 Minnis Road, Birchington, Kent CT7 9SD. Tel: 01843 841800

The Isle of Thanet is now no longer an island, though its inhabitants still consider themselves to be distinct from the rest of Kent. It is only in the past three centuries that Thanet has ceased to be an island. Before that time a channel of seawater, known as the Wantsum, cut the island off from the mainland. See Route 9 The Vanished Wantsum for details of this vanished waterway.

The Thanet village of Minster originated as a village in Roman times built on a chalk spur that projected into the Wantsum. Enter the village from the north along the lane from the A299. Find the Bell Inn by continuing along the lane, bearing slightly left in the village centre.

From the Bell Inn, walk to the Minster that gives this village its name. The minster was originally a convent founded by St Ermenburga. Young Ermenburga was niece to King Egbert I of Kent. The details are hazy, but in 673 a nobleman named Thunor murdered Ermenburga's two brothers, and King Egbert was widely held to be to blame for the killings. By way of compensation, Egbert offered Ermenburga the little village that stood on this site. She accepted, but demanded that she also get as much land as her pet hind would run round within a specified time. Egbert agreed and the deer was set loose. The hind proved to be very fleet of foot and Egbert was soon regretting his promise. Leaping on to his horse he set off to try to steer the running deer on to a shorter course. The horse shied, throwing the king into a water-filled ditch where he drowned. The hind then completed its run, having encircled 1,000 acres for Ermenburga.

Ermenburga promptly converted the land into the estate of a convent that she founded. The convent was sacked by Vikings in the 9th century so nothing of the original buildings remains standing. Most of the buildings to be seen today date to the 11th or 13th centuries. The parish church is of similar date, and was partly built with reused Roman bricks. A magnificent stained-glass window depicts the story of Ermenburga, Egbert and the hind.

Whether there is any truth in the story or not is unclear. Certainly the convent was founded by St Ermenburga with land donated by Egbert. The king did die in 673, though the circumstances are not clear. He was succeeded by his brother, Hlothere, who was murdered two years later by a nephew named Eadric. This Eadric was closely allied to the neighbouring Kingdom of Sussex, but he was killed in 688 by a cousin named Oswini who favoured an alliance to the East Saxons of Essex. Oswini was in turn ousted by Wihtred who was backed by the Franks. Turbulent times, obviously.

8

Having explored Minster, get into your car and head east along the lane towards Cliffs End. After about 2 miles find St Augustine's Cross set in a field on the right of the road, just after you pass under a railway bridge. There is a small lay-by in which to park, but there is space for only two cars so please park considerately.

This elaborately carved stone cross was erected in 1884 and dedicated to St Augustine, the Roman monk who came to Kent on a mission to convert the English to Christianity from paganism in 597. This site may be a field now, but in 597 it was a beach overlooking the Wantsum which stretched away to the south and west. Augustine landed here from a ship that was dragged up onto the beach - the sheltered waters of the Wantsum making a harbour unnecessary. Augustine brought with him 40 monks and teachers. He was welcomed here by a group of noblemen sent by King Athelbert of Kent, who conducted him to the royal capital of Canterbury. Augustine knew in advance that he would receive a reasonably warm welcome as he had been in touch with Athelbert's queen, Bertha. This Bertha was a Frankish princess and a Christian who was already worshipping at a surviving Roman church in Canterbury under her own Frankish priest. Augustine's task was to use this introduction to convert the rest of the English.

Pope Gregory had instructed Augustine to head to London, the largest city in Britain and former capital of the Roman province. However, King Sledda of Essex was determinedly pagan and opposed any increase in Frankish influence in England. He refused to let Augustine into his kingdom. Augustine accordingly stayed in Canterbury, which is why the head of the Church in England is to this day the Archbishop of Canterbury, not of London. Augustine later converted King Athelbert, and thereafter large numbers of his subjects in Kent, but failed to make much headway with the English outside of Kent. He died in 604 and was buried in the Abbey of St Peter and St Paul at Canterbury which he had founded.

9

St Augustine's Cross was erected in the 19th century to mark the spot where St Augustine landed in Kent to begin the work of converting the pagan English to the Christian religion.

From St Augustine's Cross drive east to join the A256. Turn left towards Ramsgate. At the A253 turn right to enter Ramsgate.

The town of Ramsgate is built around its old harbour and the sandy beaches nearby. The town faces south, making bathing from the beach a tempting activity on warm summer days and strolling around the town pleasant in all but the worst weather. Ramsgate became important only after Sandwich harbour silted up and most of the town dates to the early

19th century. In 1940 the harbour made a brief entry into history when it served as the reception point for the majority of ships bringing evacuated soldiers back from Dunkirk. A stained glass window in the parish church commemorates the escape of the British soldiers from the encircling German panzers.

From Ramsgate take the A255 north to drive to Broadstairs.

The town of Broadstairs is rather quieter than Ramsgate. The swimming beaches here are smaller, but pleasantly sandy and divided into a number of bays by rocky outcrops. The small harbour here was rebuilt by King Henry VIII, who also fortified the town against French invaders. Most of the town walls have since been demolished, but the York Gate remains as a stout reminder of more warlike days.

From Broadstairs take the B2052 to North Foreland where the 85-foot tall lighthouse is open at weekends. There has been a permanent light here since 1505 as the headland has long been of prime importance

The beautiful sweep of Margate Beach forms the focus for the seaside resort that sprang up in Victorian times.

as a navigational marker for ships coming up the English Channel and seeking to round Kent in order to get into London.

Continue along the B2052 into Margate, the premier resort of the Isle of Thanet.

It was the huge, curving sandy beach that made Margate attractive to Londoners seeking a holiday. When local glovemaker Benjamin Beale invented the bathing machine in 1753 he unwittingly began a revolution in leisure. Beale's machine consisted of a small wooden cabin mounted on four wheels and equipped with a set of steps. The person hiring the machine was able to get changed into a swimming costume in the privacy of the hut. The contraption was then wheeled out into the surf by the operator. The occupant could then emerge from the hut to walk down the steps into the sea. The operator, usually of the same sex as the user, was on hand to assist with any swimming lessons that were needed. Thus elegant gentlemen and ladies of fashion could enjoy sea bathing without all the tedious mucking about on the beach along with the hoi polloi. Beale's invention made sea bathing respectable for the moneyed classes. It ensured his own fortune and that of Margate.

11

These days, of course, nobody bothers with bathing machines. Most of us are happy to roll our trouser legs up to explore rock pools or get changed behind a windbreak if we fancy a dip in the sea. The seriously wealthy A-list celebs don't use a bathing machine to exclude the common herd - they jet off to Antigua instead.

The seafront at Margate has all the usual amusements on offer: candyfloss, ice creams, slot machines and the like. It also boasts a huge funfair that has been here since the 1920s. The town also boasts a grotto of ancient but unknown origin which is decorated with intricate shell designs and a network of caves in the chalk hills to the east of the beach.

Leave Margate on the A28, heading west. This main road passes through what were once the separate villages of Westbrook and Westgate, both of which have now been joined to Margate by continuous belts of housing. Just west of Westgate the A28 enters Birchington.

The shoreline here is made up of four pretty little coves separated by rocky headlands and backed by chalk cliffs. Each cove has a sandy beach and makes for pleasant bathing on warm summer days. The village centre lies a mile or so inland and is dominated by All Saints Church, a medieval construction which has in its churchyard the grave of the Victorian artist Dante Gabriel Rossetti, famous for the lush, medieval style of his paintings and poetry.

Having looked around Birchington, find Victoria's Tea Room in the village centre, just opposite the railway station.

Royal Military Canal

Start: The Swan Inn, Swan Street, Wittersham,
Kent. TN30 7PH. Tel: 01797 270 913

Finish: Little Bistro, 160a, High Street,
Hythe, Kent CT21 5JR. Tel: 01303 265393

This drive takes you into Sussex for a short while to pick up the western reaches of the Royal Military Canal, part of an elaborate system of defences constructed in the early 19th century when invasion by the French was considered a very real possibility.

In 1804 Napoleon Bonaparte was Emperor of the French. He had defeated Austria, Prussia and Russia and had reduced the small states of Italy and Germany to obeying his orders. Spain was allied to France and only Britain remained defiant. Napoleon had imposed a trade embargo on Britain and was determined to invade and conquer these islands. The main defence for Britain was, of course, the Royal Navy. But land defences were needed in case the navy failed. The Royal Military Canal was a key element in those defences.

The ports along the south coast were refortified with artillery bastions and specialised strongpoints known as Martello Towers. However, the wide, gently shelving beaches of the Romney Marsh peninsula were thought to be particularly vulnerable to a landing by French troops - and they were too extensive to be guarded along their entire length. The Royal Military Canal was an attempt to cut off the peninsula from the mainland. It was felt that although the beaches could not be held, the shorter line of the canal could. Moreover, the time taken for the French to get ashore would give the defending troops two or three days notice to march reinforcements to the canal defences. The canal was built to skirt the landward side of Romney Marsh, running at the foot of the line of low chalk hills that form the edge of the marsh.

Unlike most canals, the Royal Military Canal was not primarily for the

The Little Bistro in Hythe offers a variety of cakes, made daily by the owner's grandmother.

14

movement of barges. Instead its main purpose was to act as a heavily defended moat. Even in 1804 a water obstacle 60 feet wide and 10 feet deep was a formidable one for any army. To get an army across it complete with supply train and support forces would call for the construction of bridges, which would take several days. The sheer task of fighting across the barrier in the face of determined opposition would take some skill and great numbers, with heavy casualties an unavoidable price to be paid even if the assault were to be successful.

The earth excavated from the canal was piled up on the northern bank to form a key part of the defences. The mound was shaped so that infantry marching along the road behind it could not be seen by observers on the marsh side. Nor could the men be hit by cannonballs fired from the marsh. The top of the mound was shaped to form a firing step, allowing infantry to stand up to shoot at any advancing enemy while protected up to their chest by bullet-proof sods.

At intervals of about 500 yards the canal performed an abrupt dog leg turn before turning back to its original route. In the angle of each dog leg, the mound was shaped into an artillery emplacement. These were designed so that the cannon placed in them could fire along the length of the canal. The idea was that the cannon would mow down any troops attempting to storm over the canal, while at the same time the mound shielded the cannon from any enemy cannon firing from the marsh. No cannon were actually stationed on the canal, it being planned that they would be hauled in by horses when an invasion began.

The complex of the 28-mile long canal with its attendant earthworks and other structures cost £234,000 and employed 1,500 men to build. It was never used in action as Nelson's great naval victory at the Battle of Trafalgar gave the Royal Navy command of the seas. In 1810 the canal was opened to barge traffic as an attempt by the government to make some money out of the waterway. The canal was never terribly busy as it did not link two major cities, but did remain in use until 1909. The government then sold the eastern section to the town council of Hythe to convert into ornamental waterways and a park, while various landowners bought the rest for use in the complex drainage of Romney Marsh.

In World War II, the government commandeered the canal once again. Pill boxes and concrete gun emplacements were installed in places as the canal was converted into a gigantic tank trap to halt any attempt by German panzers to invade via the marsh. When peace came the canal was returned to civilian use.

15

A long-distance path has now been laid out along the Royal Military Canal so that walkers can stroll along all or part of the canal. The canal has become a haven for wildlife. Waterbirds such as swan, heron, kingfisher and moorhen are common here. The margins have become colonised by plants such as yellow flag, water lily and bladderwort. These shelter a multitude of insects, including dragonflies, glow-worms and mayfly. The patient observer might glimpse shy mammals such as the watervole or mink.

From the Swan Inn, drive east along Swan Street to reach a T-junction with the B2082. Turn right heading south along the B2082 toward Iden and Rye. In Iden turn left along the lane to Houghton Green, bearing left again to come to a T-junction with a lane. Rye is to the right, but turn left towards Appledore.

The waterway on your right is the River Rother, which along this stretch

The defensive capabilities of the Royal Military Canal were brought to the fore for a second time in 1940. Just south of Appledore a concrete pillbox was erected on the site of an original artillery position.

formed part of the Royal Military Canal defensive network. Where the lane crosses over the River Rother, the Royal Military Canal proper cuts off to head northeast. Continue along the lane. This section of lane is the military road built alongside the canal to allow troops to march along the canal to any point threatened by an attacker. At Appledore turn right along the B2080 towards Snargate.

This road cuts across Romney Marsh and gives a good idea of the lonely stretches of pastureland that existed here in Napoleonic times. The marsh was a real marsh until the 18th century when determined efforts to drain the land and make it productive were begun. The drainage continued into the 19th century and today a complex pattern of drains, dykes and canals criss-cross the area. These take away water in wet weather, then bring it back again in summer droughts to ensure that the lush pasture ground continues to produce tasty and nutritious grass whatever the weather. The Royal Military Canal now performs a vital role in this system as it is in the canal that winter rainfall is stored for use in the summer.

Technically there are two marshes here. Romney Marsh proper lies to the north and east of the B2080 and the causeway on which it runs. To the south and west stretches the Walland Marsh, large areas of which remain only poorly drained to this day.

Continue through Snargate to Brenzett. Turn left along the A2070 to Warehorne. At Warehorne turn right along the B2067 towards Hythe. This road again follows the line of the old military road, but here it is some distance from the Royal Military Canal itself which is only occasionally to be seen to the right of the road.

In Hythe the Royal Military Canal forms a major feature of the town. It has been converted into ornamental water features and is surrounded by landscaped gardens. Boats are usually for hire if you fancy splashing

17

The impressive monument that stands in Hythe alongside the Royal Military Canal. The figures are of soldiers from the time that the canal was built, while the board gives information about the canal.

In Hythe the Royal Military Canal has been converted into ornamental water features.

about a bit. The old town centre lies to the north of the canal, while the more modern seaside resort areas are to the south. Both parts of Hythe are worth a visit, though they are very different from each other.

If you wish to continue with the Napoleonic theme, you should walk to the western end of the sand-shingle beach to find the Martello Tower that was erected here to guard the beach against a French landing. The Martello Towers were built at the same time as the Royal Military Canal to guard vulnerable stretches of coastline. They were named after the fort at Martella in southern Italy which held off an attack by the Royal Navy in 1794. Each consisted of a round stone tower about 40 feet tall with massively thick walls. The tower was topped by a gun platform on which was mounted a heavy cannon on a revolving slide that allowed it to fire in any direction. Each was manned by one officer and 20 men.

18

Having inspected the Martello Tower, you should return to Hythe high street where the Little Bistro will be found right at the eastern end. The shop is run by a young lady, and the cakes are all home-made by her grandmother - and they are truly delicious.

The Swan Inn is a traditional country pub specialising in real ale, real cider for which they have won numerous "Camra" (campaign for real ale) awards and traditional good value pub food. Family and dog friendly, with a saloon bar, public bar and separate restaurant. Hours are: 11.00am - 12.00am Monday - Thursday. 11.00am - 2.00am Friday and Saturday and 12.00pm - 12.00am Sundays. Food is served from 12.00 - 3.00pm and 6.00pm - 9.00pm Monday - Friday. 12.00pm - 9.00pm Saturday and 12.00pm - 4.00pm and 7.00pm - 9.00pm Sundays.

Eden Valley

Start: The Swan Inn, Swan Lane, Marlpit Hill, Edenbridge, Kent TN8 6BA. Tel: 01732 862313

Finish: Quaintways Tea Rooms, High Street, Penshurst, Tonbridge, Kent TN11 8BT. Tel: 01892 870272

The Eden Valley is almost as idyllic as its name might suggest. There is no real Garden of Eden here, but the gentle valley does include some of the most pleasant countryside in the county that has rightly been called the Garden of England. The Eden rises in Surrey, so this route takes you just over the border to view the headwaters before returning to Kent for most of the route.

The Swan Inn lies north of Edenbridge proper in Marlpit Hill, which was once a separate village but has now run together with Edenbridge as housing has expanded. Find The Swan just off the high street about 50 yards north of the railway station.

The gatehouse to Hever Castle, one of the most enchanting stately homes in Kent.

The execution of Anne Boleyn as imagined by a Victorian artist. Anne grew up at Hever and her ghost is said to haunt the area.

Leave The Swan and head south along the B2026 to Edenbridge. It is worth stopping here to view the eponymous bridge over the Eden. **About a mile south of Edenbridge, turn right along the B2028 through Marsh Green and Dormansland to reach Lingfield.** This small town is famous for its racecourse, but the 15th century Church of St Peter and St Paul is open more often and has more to offer the visitor than a way to gamble. When this church was rebuilt, the tombs of the earlier church were retained. Of particular interest are the tombs of the 1st, 2nd and 3rd Baron Cobham dating from 1361, 1403 and 1446 respectively. Each shows their occupant dressed in battle armour and allows historians to track changes in the armour of a medieval knight during these years.

From Lingfield head northwest on the B2029 toward Blindley Heath. Before reaching the junction with the A22 the road crosses the headwaters of the Eden by way of a small bridge - the

river here is little more than a large culvert to be honest - which it is easy to miss. Having viewed this small stream, head back towards Lingfield but before reaching the village turn left along the lane to Haxted and Edenbridge. Entering Edenbridge turn right along the B2026, then very quickly left along the lane signposted to Hever.

The main attraction at Hever is, of course, Hever Castle. This is not so much a castle as a fortified manor house that was rebuilt in the 15th century to be a comfortable country house with ornamental turrets and castellations - it was not intended to be a serious fortification and never saw any fighting. Hever entered history as the childhood home of Anne Boleyn, who was later to become the second wife of King Henry VIII.

Anne was pretty, intelligent and fervently interested in the religious debates that were wracking Europe as the Reformation took hold. Henry became infatuated with her at a time when it was becoming clear that his queen, Catherine of Aragon, was not going to be able to produce the male heir that Henry needed to secure the Tudor dynasty on the throne. Henry's subsequent divorce from Catherine and marriage to Anne were instrumental in bringing the Reformation to England which thereafter became a staunchly Protestant nation. Anne gave Henry a daughter, later Queen Elizabeth I, but two miscarriages convinced Henry that she would not produce a son. Her subsequent trial for adultery is generally believed to have been fixed by Henry. She was executed on 19 May 1536.

Perhaps predictably Anne Boleyn's ghost is said to haunt Hever Castle, being seen most often around Christmas time. Perhaps she returns here to a place where she was so happy in life.

Henry confiscated Hever from the Boleyn family and later sold the estate. The house was never again inhabited by a grand family, being used as an estate office by absentee landlords and later as a farmhouse. It was bought in the early 20th century by the American millionaire William Waldorf Astor who restored the house to its Tudor splendour. Astor also laid out the splendid gardens, and this work involved diverting the Eden an impressive 200 yards to the north where it is dammed to form a vast 35-acre lake. The grounds also include a maze, a feature much loved in Tudor times, together with an Italianate garden, a Tudor garden and fine collection of statues and busts.

Leave Hever heading north along the lane to Bough Beech. At the junction with the B2027 turn right towards Chiddingstone. At Chiddingstone turn right along the B2176 towards Penshurst. As you enter the village you will see the magnificent stately home of Penshurst Place set back from the road on the left. There is a signed car park and, since parking in the village centre is severely limited, it is wise to park here.

The centre of the village is highly picturesque and well worth a stroll. Of particular interest is the lych-house. This peculiar building was built in the later 16th century and takes the form of a two-storey house that straddles the lych gate into the churchyard. It is a private home and is not open, but is worth a look at the outside. The church itself is largely 14th century, though parts of the 12th century church remain, with a 17th century tower. Off to one side is the private chapel of the Sydney family of nearby Penshurst Place. The chapel is richly decorated, with an especially fine ceiling.

22

Penshurst Place stands just outside Penshurst and is one of the largest of the grand houses of Kent.

Penshurst Place itself was begun in 1340 for Sir John de Pulteney. Pulteney was a wealthy wool merchant who rose to be Lord Mayor of London and built Penshurst to be his country retreat. The house was massively enlarged in Tudor times by the Sydneys and has been kept in good condition by them ever since. The house is open to the public daily throughout the summer, but opening times in the winter can vary so it is as well to check the website on www.penshurstplace.com before setting out.

Once you have had a good look round Penshurst, you should head for the High Street where Quaintways Tea Rooms are to be found. Quaintways are not open on a Monday, and in winter close at 4.30pm rather than at 5.30pm as in the summer.

24

The village centre of Penshurst is crowded with ancient cottages and buildings that lend a picturesque charm to the place.

The Teise Valley

Start: The Bull Inn, Linton Hill, Linton, Maidstone, Kent ME17 4AW. Tel: 01622 743612

Finish: Weeks Tea Rooms, 12, High Street, Goudhurst, Kent TN17 1AG. Tel: 01580 211380

The Teise is one of the major tributaries of the Medway, itself one of the two key rivers of Kent, the other being the Stour. The Teise is highly unusual in that it splits in two to flow around a ridge of high ground, then joins together again to enter the Medway - effectively this flow creates an inland island surrounded by river water. The two branches of the Teise are known as the Greater Teise and Lesser Teise, but the names are misleading. Since a land improvement scheme in the mid-20th century led to the drainage of large areas of water meadow in the valley, the Greater Teise has actually carried considerably less water than the Lesser Teise. Were it not for the fact that the River Beult enters the Greater Teise near Chainhurst it would be an insignificant stream indeed.

Find the The Bull on the main north-south road (A229) through Linton. Leave the pub heading north along the main road. At the junction with the B2163 turn left to head west through Coxheath. At the junction with the B2010 a couple of miles past Coxheath, turn left to head south to Yalding. In the village pause to inspect the bridge over the Greater Teise. The Beult has already joined the stream at this point, which accounts for the larger amount of water that is usually present. A short distance to the west is the confluence with the Medway. Once over this bridge you are on the "island" of land surrounded by the two branches of the Teise.

About 300 yards past the bridge, turn left along the B2162 through Benover and Mockbeggar. At Claygate the road crosses the Lesser Teise then continues on to The Corner and Hazel Street. At the roundabout junction with the A21 continue

The vineyards at Lamberhurst were first planted in 1972, making them among the oldest in England.

straight across on to the B2162. After about 2 miles you will reach Lamberhurst Down

Lamberhurst vineyards are among the oldest in England, having been founded in 1972 as the climate was recovering from the cold period that had lasted for the previous couple of centuries. There is a shop on site that sells wine made here, but there is much else to see as well. There is a guided tour of the vineyard, winemaking facilities and other working aspects of the business - this takes about 45 minutes to complete. In good weather you may care to buy one of the hampers on offer in the shop to enjoy a picnic in the extensive grounds. Visitors are also welcome to stroll around by themselves. Various special events are held throughout the year, see the website www.lamberhurstvineyard.net for details.

Unusually among English vineyards, the vines at Lamberhurst are planted on a north-facing slope. This means they receive rather less summer sun, but given the special microclimate in this corner of the Teise Valley it also makes them less prone to spring frosts when a cold snap could wipe out the entire crop. The grapes grown here are mainly of the bacchus, pinot noir, rondo, regent and Ortega varieties, though other more specialist grapes are produced in small quantities.

Leaving Lamberhurst Vineyard, head west along the B2169.

After some three miles or so a lane on the right will be signposted to Bayham Abbey.

The remains at Bayham Abbey are among the finest medieval ruins in Kent. Although most of what is to be seen here today is genuinely medieval, the ruins did get a makeover in the 18th century when they were included in an extensive garden landscaped by society gardener Humphrey Repton. Although today less well known than his older contemporary "Capability" Brown, Repton was arguably more influential in his day due to the publication of his monumental work "Observations on the Theory and Practice of Landscape Gardening" in 1803. Repton delighted in what he termed the "picturesque" qualities of a garden and liked nothing better than constructing views that might have looked good as landscape paintings. His work at Bayham used the ruins, with suitably romantic embellishments, as the focus for several vistas.

Having viewed the ruins at Bayham, return to the B2169 and drive east. Take the first on the left to pass Hoathly Farm, then turn right towards Lamberhurst and find a lane to the Owl House on the left. The house itself is a 16th century cottage that once served as the headquarters for a gang of smugglers. The building is not open, but the extensive grounds are open to the public. The true glory of these gardens are the roses, so it is best to visit in the summer months.

27

From the Owl House head east towards Lamberhurst to rejoin the B2162. Turn left to return to the roundabout junction with the A21. This time head right along the A262 towards Goudhurst and Cranbrook. At Goudhurst the road climbs up out of the Teise valley, here carpeted with orchards, to reach the summit of a hill that forms the drainage divide between the valleys of the Teise and Beult.

This village underwent an economic boom in the later medieval period when the locals took up weaving woollen cloth. Many of the houses and other buildings in the village date from this time. The church was rebuilt in the mid-1400s in grand style - though the tower is some two centuries younger and was completed in the then fashionable Renaissance style which is quite unlike the Gothic architecture of the rest of the church.

Inside the church is the tomb of Sir Alexander Culpeper, who died in 1537, and his wife. The Culpepers were the major landowners of this area for centuries and their tombs are significant features in many of the churches hereabouts. This particular tomb is unusual in that it is made of wood, painted in lifelike colours to show Sir Alexander and his wife as if they had just nodded off to sleep for a while.

When you have completed a gentle stroll around the village head for the High Street. You will find the welcoming Weeks Tea Rooms at number 12. These tea rooms are closed on Wednesday afternoons and Sundays during the winter months. They are certainly worth making the effort to visit as I have never seen such a variety of cakes, the lady who runs the shop told me that she generally has 40 varieties on offer.

The village of Goudhurst centres around the main street that clambers up a steep hill with the church at the top.

29

This drive ends at Weeks Tea Rooms in Goudhurst, which offers a fine range of cakes and savouries.

If you have time after tea you might care to drive south along the B2079 toward Stonecrouch. The National Pinetum is off this road about three miles south of Goudhurst. The Pinetum has much to offer those interested in pine trees - and for the rest of us it makes for a peaceful place for a stroll to work off a sumptuous helping of cakes and scones.

30

The Red Lion at Snargate stands in a rather lonely position in the midst of the Romney Marsh.

The Isle of Oxney

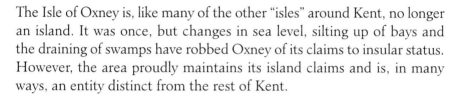

Start: The Rose & Crown, Swamp Road, Old Romney,
Romney Marsh, Kent, TN29 9SQ. Tel: 01797 367500

Finish: Sandhurst Tea Rooms, Queen Street,
Sandhurst, Kent TN18 5HY. Tel: 01580 850745

The Isle of Oxney is, like many of the other "isles" around Kent, no longer an island. It was once, but changes in sea level, silting up of bays and the draining of swamps have robbed Oxney of its claims to insular status. However, the area proudly maintains its island claims and is, in many ways, an entity distinct from the rest of Kent.

The "isle" covers the area of land that lies between the River Rother, the Royal Military Canal and the damp lowlands west of Kenardington. The villages of Wittersham, The Stocks, Stone and Small Hythe are the main population centres of Oxney. This drive takes in most of the "isle", but also embraces some nearby areas.

In Roman times, Oxney really was an island. The sea level was then about ten feet or so higher in relation to the coast of southern England than it is today. Most of what is now Romney Marsh was then tidal mud flats while Walland Marsh was mostly underwater. Seawater washed against the east, south and west of the Isle of Oxney, with the coast stretching as far inland to what is now Hawkhurst and Robertsbridge. To the north Oxney was cut off from the mainland by an area of salt marsh through which meandered the estuary of the Rother. By 1250 sea levels had fallen so that Romney Marsh had become a marsh while Walland was tidal flats. The Rother still ran north of Oxney, entering the sea at what is now Old Romney, then a busy port. The south, east and west sides of Oxney were bordered by tidal salt marshes.

In 1287 a major storm struck. The town of Winchelsea was washed away completely - the village of that name being built on a nearby hill after the storm. Broomhill was likewise swept away, but not rebuilt. The

Rother changed its course as a result of the storm, now flowing south of Oxney to enter the sea near Rye, as it still does today. Old Romney was finished as a port and now lies some miles inland. These changes marked the end of Oxney as an island. The old course of the Rother north of the island was drained to become productive grazing land by around 1600, with the marshy land to the south and east following by 1750. By 1800 the remaining marshes had been drained and Oxney was an isle no more.

The drive starts at the The Rose & Crown in Old Romney. It stands just off the A259 in the village centre. This village stands in the area between Romney Marsh to the east and Walland Marsh to the south. If you look southwest you will see in the distance - on a clear day - the hill, formerly an island, on which stands the port-town of Rye. Visible to the southeast is a small rise in the ground where Old Romney stands. Directly north can be seen a low chalk escarpment, the former coastline. To the northwest is a line of low hills that form the Isle of Oxney. The flat land all around you is now occupied by pasture land, but was formerly mud flats and open sea.

32

Leave Old Romney heading north along the A259. At a roundabout go straight over to join the B2080. Just past the scattered village of Snargate, turn right along the lane to Warehorne. This lane strikes out across the Romney Marsh that was tidal flats in Roman times. Archaeologists have found traces of salt pans here. At Warehorne it is worth pausing to find the redbrick Church Farm next to the church. This was formerly the rectory and was home to Richard H. Barham during the time that he was vicar here.

Barham had seemed set on a steady if unspectacular career as a member of the minor landed gentry until in 1802 the coach he was travelling in overturned and he was almost killed. After a prolonged recuperation, Barham turned to the Church and was ordained in 1813. From his quiet rectory here in Warehorne he penned a series of short stories, poems and novels under the pseudonym of Thomas Ingoldsby. The most famous of these were the three volumes of humorous and satirical tales published as the Ingoldsby Legends. He died in 1844, after which the true identity of Thomas Ingoldsby was revealed.

Church Farm at Warehorne was once home to Victorian novelist Richard H. Barham, author of the Ingoldsby Legends.

Continue straight through Warehorne to reach the B2067. Turn left to Tenterden. This road runs along what was once the mainland coastline. To your left was the estuary of the Rother, an area of swamp and salt-marsh beyond which lay the Isle of Oxney. **At Tenterden turn left on the A28, then within a hundred yards or so left again on to the B2082 to Small Hythe.**

On this road you will pass the famous Tenterden Vineyards, home to the Chapel Down family of wines. The vineyard is open daily June to September and at weekends in May and October, with the shop only being open in the winter months. The vineyards cover 25 acres of generally south-facing slopes on which are grown Bacchus, Pinot Noir, Dornfelder, Pinot Blanc and Chardonnay grapes among others.

When you reach Small Hythe itself you will see brown National Trust signs for Smallhythe Place. This is a pretty 16th century house boasting a rose garden, nut orchard and wildflower garden, but its main attraction

Smallhythe Place is a 16th century house that was home to Dame Ellen Terry, the great Victorian actress. It is now owned by the National Trust.

is its link to Dame Ellen Terry. This great Victorian actress went on the London stage at the age of 8 in 1856 and by 1868 was already a well-known star. She took a ten year break to have her children, but was back on the stage by 1878 when she began to specialise in Shakespearean works. It is generally reckoned that she dominated the English stage for some 20 years, and played to packed houses in America as well. In 1903 she turned to theatre management, encouraging several young, rising stars in their careers. She lived here from 1899 to her death in 1928. The house contains a wide-ranging collection of artefacts and ephemera relating to both Ellen Terry herself and to the Victorian theatre.

From Small Hythe continue along the B2082 through Wittersham and The Stocks. At The Stocks the B2082 turns sharp right, but you should continue straight on along the lane to Stone. This village stands on the southeastern tip of Oxney and once looked out across the open sea toward France. Today it offers fine views over Walland Marsh towards the distant nuclear power station at Dungeness.

Return along the lane to The Stocks and turn left along the B2082 towards Rye. This road dips down off the Isle of Oxney and on to what are known as the Rother Levels. This broad, flat valley was among the last stretches of marshland in this area to be drained. It is still muddy after rain and in the winter. The road crosses the River Rother then passes through the little village of Iden. **At the junction with the A268 turn right and stay on this road through Peasmarsh and Newenden towards Sandhurst.** You will find the charming Sandhurst Tea Rooms just past the traffic lights on the left-hand side of the road in the centre of the village.

These tearooms are a real find. Everything on offer is home-made and ranges from scones and cakes to light lunches and sandwiches. There is a charming little garden with a gazebo, water feature and terrace. The Sandhurst Tea Rooms are generally open all year round but closed on Monday and Tuesday.

35

The delicious cream tea served at the Sandhurst Tea Rooms in Sandhurst.

The monument on the banks of the River Medway which commemorates the battle fought here in AD43 between the invading Romans and the native Britons.

The Battle Gap

Start: The Watermans Arms, 151, High Street, Wouldham, Rochester, Kent ME1 3TY. Tel: 01634 861503

Finish: The Old Mill Tea Room Ltd, Mill Yard, Swan Street, West Malling, Kent ME19 6LP. Tel: 01732 844311

The wide River Medway with its broad, marshy valley and extensive flood plain cuts south across Kent from the Thames estuary to Tonbridge, where its headwaters rise in the Weald. Until recently the Weald was an area of thick forests standing on damp clay soils that were almost impassable in winter or wet weather. The Medway thus formed a distinctive and very real barrier to movement from east to west. So clear was this dividing line that folk on one side of the river called themselves Kentish men, while those on the other termed themselves men of Kent.

37

The river was no less a barrier to the movement of armies, so crossing points have long been a key strategic aim for any army operating in the area. The Romans built a bridge over the Medway at what is now Rochester. That crossing point was retained in good condition through the centuries that followed and in medieval times was guarded by the massive Rochester Castle, the ruins of which are still among the most impressive in England. This drive takes in three key battlefields which determined the outcomes of three very different wars.

Find the Watermans Arms in Wouldham on the main street just south of the church. On leaving the pub drive south along the High Street to find the battlefield of the Medway Battle, fought in AD43 during the Roman invasion of Britain. The Roman army led by the general Aulus Plautius consisted of three legions, the IX Hispania, the XIV Gemina and the XX Valeria, plus a number of auxiliary units and cavalry forces - probably around 35,000 combat troops, plus a number of support and administrative personnel. This army landed at Richborough, secured the harbour at Reculver for their supply ships then headed west along the chalk ridge of the North Downs until they found their route blocked by the Medway. Plautius had left troops behind to garrison Reculver and other places, so he may have had 30,000 men with him on the day of battle.

On the far bank stood an army raised by the Celtic King Caractacus of the Catuvellauni tribe with his various allies. He had an army considerably larger than that of the Romans, perhaps 50,000 men. He seems to have put his main force on the bank more or less opposite Wouldham. There was a ford here in those days, long since dredged out to make the Medway navigable.

The battle began before dawn when Plautius sent a force of Batavian troops down river to swim across. The Batavians came from the lower Rhine and were skilled in river crossings. Plautius seems to have hoped to get these men around the left flank of the British. The move failed as the men were seen and Caractacus sent a force off to attack them. Plautius then moved most of his army forward as if hoping to force the

38

ford. In fact this was a diversion, for the II Augusta under its commander Vespasian (later to be emperor of Rome) was marching south through woods to cross the Medway further upstream. The II Augusta got over the river safely, but by this time it was dusk and the incoming tide cut Vespasian off from any reinforcement.

At dawn Caractacus attacked. It was a bloody engagement and was nearly a defeat for the Romans, but the tide fell just in time and Plautius was able to push the remaining two legions over the river. Caractacus retreated from the Medway. The defeat proved to be decisive. The tribes allied to Caractacus melted away to make separate peace treaties with Rome. There would be other battles in the years to come, but never again did the Romans look likely to be pushed out of Britain.

Drive south along the lane to the village of Burham. Turn right to the smaller village of Burham Court. A footpath beside the old church here leads to the banks of the Medway. If you are feeling energetic you could walk north along the river bank to find the monument erected in the 20th century to mark the spot where Vespasian crossed the river. The river today flows between embankments and most of what was the marshy floodplain has been drained. The landscape is quite different from that faced by the Romans, but this is still a bleak and largely uninhabited area.

From Burham drive south to Aylesford. In the village find the church on a small hill just north of the Medway and the old bridge that spans the river here. Although the bridge is some centuries old, this was originally a ford over the Medway and it was for control of this ford that the Battle of Aylesford was fought in 455.

After the Roman army abandoned Britain in 410, the locals were left to defend themselves against increasingly serious raids from the Irish, Picts and Saxons. The locals elected a senior governor to be their military leader, giving him the title of Vortigern. In addition to strengthening town walls and recruiting local men into a new army, Vortigern hired a pair of Saxon mercenaries named Hengist and Horsa, who were probably brothers, to defend the coastline with their force of tough men and swift ships.

39

The bridge at Aylesford built on the site of the ancient ford where a battle was fought in about 455 that decided the fate of Britain.

This period of British history is termed the Dark Ages for few contemporary accounts survive and to reconstruct the events of the time historians rely on later accounts and fragmentary contemporary references. It is particularly difficult to assign firm dates to events. See Drive 13 for details of the events at this time. In about 455, the Romano-British invaded Kent under the leadership of Vortigern's sons Vortimer and Categirn. The invasion began well but they found themselves blocked at the Medway by Hengist and Horsa. The attackers decided to force the river crossing at Aylesford.

Details of the fighting are sparse, but there seem to have been about 4,000 men on each side. The Saxon army would have consisted largely of infantry armed with spears, knives and shields. Only the richer men would have had swords and helmets. The Romano-Britons would have had infantry equipped in broadly similar fashion, but their most effective troops were the heavily-armoured cavalry. Those cavalry needed open country to be really useful, which was probably why the Saxons sought to halt the invasion at this cramped river crossing.

Exactly what happened we don't know, but the battle ended with Horsa and Categirn both dead. Vortimer then retreated, leaving Hengist as the victor of the battlefield. Hengist took his brother's body up to the hill overlooking the battlefield and buried it there. He then set up a great boulder to mark the spot - it is still there but the climb there and back is both arduous and difficult to describe. Hengist painted the rock red and then added a prancing white horse. The symbol has remained that of Kent to this day.

As with the Roman battle fought to the north, the conflict at Aylesford was important as it failed to dislodge an invader. Hengist sent back to Germany for reinforcements, which came flooding over in vast numbers. The resulting war would take several generations to complete, but by around the year 600 most of what is now England was in the hands of the Angles and Saxons who, together with some defeated Britons who stayed in the conquered lands, gave rise to the English nation.

The final battle on this route was a success for the attacker. **From Aylesford drive southeast to Maidstone, then leave that town on**

The Roundheads seeking to attack Royalist Maidstone launched a surprise assault over the bridge at East Farleigh that outflanked the Royalist defences and brought them a swift victory.

the B2010 towards Yalding and Tunbridge Wells. About three miles from Maidstone town centre the road passes through East Farleigh. At a crossroads by the church in the village centre turn right to drop down a steep hill to the old medieval bridge over the Medway. This was the scene of battle in 1648.

During the English Civil War between King Charles and Parliament, the people of Kent were evenly divided in their loyalties. The county was, however, of prime strategic importance. The Channel ports were vital, while the naval forces based at Chatham were in a position to blockade the Thames and so stop all ships heading for London. Having the capital city as their headquarters, the military forces of Parliament could not afford to let Kent fall into Royalist hands. Consequently 2,400 Roundheads led by Colonel Sandys marched into the county as soon as hostilities began in the summer of 1642. The Royalists in the county lacked any local leaderships, so Sandys was able to secure the key towns and fortresses of the county without trouble. He held Kent for the rest of the hostilities, which came to an end with Parliamentary victory in 1646.

On Christmas Day 1647, however, rioting broke out in Canterbury as local Royalists objected to the Parliamentarian troops flaunting their victory. The Roundheads were driven out after some hours of savage street fighting. The Parliamentarians were soon back, along with 3,000 reinforcements from London and some cannon. A long section of Canterbury's city walls were destroyed by way of discouraging any future trouble and those citizens deemed to have been ringleaders were marched off to prison in Leeds Castle. The event, and the reaction of the Kentish folk to it, convinced the Earl of Norwich that a properly organised uprising would attract much support in the county. He began laying his plans.

A Celtic warrior equipped as the Britons would have been at the Battle of the Medway as they sought to halt the Roman invasion.

The plans in Kent were encouraged by the fact that in March South Wales rose in rebellion, and by April was successfully holding off the Parliamentarian troops sent to defeat them. Then in April the Scottish Parliament demanded that King Charles be sent north to rule them. If England did not want the king, Scotland did. The Scottish army was mustered for an invasion of England, more Roundhead troops marched north to face them. In May, Norwich struck and he set Kent afire with action.

He made his headquarters in Maidstone and sent riders galloping out across the county summoning all loyal subjects of King Charles to come to join him. Some of those who marched into Maidstone were professional soldiers, others had had some form of military training, others were novices. Many had modern weapons, others carried only farm axes or hunting guns. It was a mixed force of uneven quality, but within two weeks it was over 10,000 strong.

Norwich sent one force off to Dover under Sir Richard Hardress. The town was captured, but the castle held out, so Hardress began a siege. Another column was sent to Rochester to secure the bridge over the Medway, a task achieved with ease. The Rochester column marched on to Upnor, capturing the castle there from its Roundhead garrison without much difficulty. A third force marched to Deal Castle, Sandown Castle and Walmer Castle, capturing all three after only brief fighting. Norwich's greatest triumph came when several naval ships at Chatham declared for the king and put to sea. Norwich used the ships to get in touch with the Royalists in Wales and Scotland and to establish links with the exiled prince who was later to be King Charles II.

To deal with this dangerous uprising, Parliament sent Sir Thomas Fairfax and 6,000 men of the New Model Army. Fairfax was, after Cromwell, the finest soldier in England at the time, while the New Model Army was composed of fully-trained professional troops armed with the very latest and most effective weaponry available. It was a formidable force, so Norwich wisely decided to stand on the defensive. He hoped to slow down the Parliamentarian advance while the more effective Royalist forces in Wales and Scotland got into action. If he could tie down Fairfax and his men, Norwich knew that he would play a major role in Royalist success. Norwich put detachments at every bridge and ford over the Medway and prepared to move his army from Maidstone to any threatened spot.

43

Fairfax recognised Norwich's strategy and knew that his task was to defeat the Kentish royalists as quickly as possible so that he could take his men to face the more serious threats elsewhere. He began by sending a force to invest Upnor, the only Royalist outpost west of the Medway. He then sent scouts out to reconnoitre the Medway and its crossing points. They came back to report that the main Royalist army was in Maidstone, with detachments holding all the bridges and fords.

Fairfax marched his main army up to the bridge at Maidstone at dawn on 1 June. He made a show of reconnoitring the heavily-defended crossing, then marched off north as if heading for the bridge at Aylesford. In fact, it was a ruse. As soon as he was out of sight of the Royalists, Fairfax altered direction and headed southwest to the bridge at East Farleigh. He attacked at noon in overwhelming force. The Royalist garrison put up a brave resistance, but they were soon either killed or swept away. In the 1860s builders found the pit in which the bodies of the dead had been thrown.

A Roman legionary of AD47. The Romans were not noticeably better armed than the Celts, but their disciplined tactics assured them of victory.

Fairfax marched on swiftly to attack Maidstone from the south, while Norwich was looking north. The assault began at 7pm and within an hour the Roundheads had broken through the barricades and ditches to get into the town. The street fighting lasted until midnight and culminated in the defence of St Faith's Church by Norwich and his men. There could be no denying the assault of Fairfax and his professionals, however, and long before dawn the surviving Royalists were fleeing out of the town.

The Kentish campaign was over so far as open campaigning was concerned. However, the Royalists were determined to keep Fairfax busy, so the captured castles defied him. Rochester fell first, then Sandown and Deal. Walmer was the last to surrender, on 12 July.

Having inspected the bridge and battlefield at East Farleigh, cross over the bridge and drive north up the lane for about a mile to reach the A26. Turn left. After about three miles you will reach the junction with the A228 at Mereworth. Turn right along the A228. After another two miles bear left along the lane signposted to West Malling.

The High Street of West Malling has some impressive Tudor and Stuart houses, several of them converted into shops. The church has one of the largest Norman towers in Kent. You may care to have a look around before heading for the Old Mill Tea Room in Mill Yard, just off Swan Street. Swan Street can be found by walking north along the High Street from the church for about 150 yards and turning right. The cakes here are truly lovely, being baked on the premises and light lunches are served until 3pm. The Old Mill is not generally open on a Sunday, though it does open during the Christmas Lights season and if there is some special event on in the town.

Smugglers Marsh

Start: Dolphin Inn Hotel, 11, South Street, Lydd,
Romney Marsh, Kent TN29 9DQ. Tel: 01797 320259

Finish: Lathe Barn Tea Rooms, Donkey Street, Burmarsh,
Romney Marsh, Kent TN29 0JN. Tel: 01303 873618

Romney Marsh, and its southern neighbour Walland Marsh, forms perhaps the most distinctive of all Kent landscapes. The vast flat lands offer sweeping views in all directions and a rare opportunity in England to see the 'big sky' more often associated with the open sea. This drive weaves around the marshes to take in most of the sights.

Both Romney Marsh and Walland Marsh originated as extensive mud flats off the coast. In Roman times they were both largely underwater, but over the following centuries a combination of falling sea levels and determined efforts at land reclamation converted the area into prime sheep grazing land. The drained marshes now have a higher density of sheep than anywhere else in Britain and, other than a couple of areas in New Zealand, than anywhere in the world.

45

Most sheep here are of the local Romney Marsh breed. This breed was developed in the 18th century and formalised in the 19th century from the local sheep already grazing here. The sheep have relatively short legs and heavy bodies. It is noted for its excellent meat, but is also a useful producer of wool with fleeces averaging 10lb on ewes and 17lb on rams. The wool has a long staple, making it suitable for weaving into worsted cloths for suits. The distinctive feature of the breed, however, is that it is resistant to foot infections from which other breeds would suffer if put out to graze on the damp soils of the area.

The town of Lydd, where this drive begins, stands on the B2075 off the A259 on the southern flank of Walland Marsh. The area originated as an offshore island in Roman times, but by the early Middle Ages was an island surrounded by marsh. In 798 the island was the scene of a savage battle that saw the end of Kent as an independent kingdom. Over the previous half century, the Kings of Kent had periodically acknowledged that the kings of the powerful Midlands kingdom of Mercia were their overlords, but the relationship had always been loose and poorly defined. In 796 King Edbrit Praen of Kent threw off the overlordship of Mercia and declared himself independent.

Two years later King Cenwulf of Mercia marched into Kent to put an end to such presumption. He brought with him a large army, so large that the Kent forces could not hope to win an open battle. Edbrit Praen began a guerrilla war, ambushing Mercian patrols, attacking supply wagons and seeking to make the campaign more trouble than it was worth for Cenwulf. Unfortunately for Edbrit Praen, Cenwulf discovered that he was organising resistance from his base on the island of Lydd. The Mercians marched down to attack.

The fighting probably centred around the causeway over the marsh that followed the route that is now the B2075. Details of the action were not recorded in the contemporary chronicles. We know only that Edbrit Praen was captured, had his hands cut off and was condemned to death. Cenwulf had his own brother Cuthred crowned King of Kent at Canterbury. This Mercian prince ruled until his death in 807, but Kentish independence was a mirage, the kingdom had become little more than a province of Mercia.

In Lydd you will find the Dolphin Hotel on South Street off the High Street beside the church.

While in Lydd it is worth paying a visit to the large parish church. A few fragments of wall in the church date back to the time of the battle, but it was almost completely rebuilt in Norman times and was altered again in the 13th century. Some rebuilding was necessary after a German bomb struck the church during World War II. If the tower is open, it is worth the strenuous climb for the views on offer across the marshes.

From Lydd head southwest on the lane to Camber. The sandy beach at Camber is several miles long, so if the weather is nice you might care to go for a paddle or buy an ice cream. Pass through Camber to emerge on to the A259 at East Guldeford. The church here is usually locked and rarely used. From the outside it looks rather like a barn, but inside it has magnificent box pews and a fine pulpit.

Turn right onto the A259 and follow it across the open expanses of Walland Marsh to the villages of Brookland and Brenzett. As the A259 reaches Brenzett it reaches a roundabout junction with the A2070. A lane off this roundabout is signposted to the Brenzett Aeronautical Museum. This museum

The magnificent tower of the church at Lydd offers stunning views over the surrounding marshes, and out to sea toward France.

47

is open weekends and bank holidays during the summer and at other times for special events - you can phone them on 01797 344747 for details before you set off if you like.

The museum is housed in buildings that originally formed part of the RAF fighter base built here in 1942. There are numerous exhibits from the RAF days, plus a monument to all those who served here. The museum houses a wide range of exhibits, with a special section dedicated to the highly dangerous task of bomb disposal. Pride of place, however, goes to the original Dambuster bomb which was made for the famous 1943 raid by RAF bombers on the Ruhr dams that were so vital to Germany's war industries. In the event this spare bomb was never used and so found its way here.

The Ship Inn at Dymchurch includes a secret room, rediscovered during recent renovations and now equipped with a waxwork smuggler.

From the Brenzett roundabout, continue along the A259. The road will pass through Old Romney. This little village was once a bustling and busy port on the coast where the River Rother entered the sea. As the sea level dropped the coast retreated to the south, so eventually the merchants and sailors abandoned the port at Old Romney to build a new one at New Romney, further along the A259.

New Romney was in its turn abandoned when the Rother changed its course and is now likewise some distance from the sea. The church of St Nicholas was erected in the town's heyday and has some fine stained-glass windows. The town's main fame lies in the fact that it is recognised as being the capital of Romney Marsh and for many years was a centre for smugglers.

The most famous smuggler of Romney Marsh was a character who never actually existed. Dr Syn was a fictional smuggler invented by local author Russell Thorndike for a series of novels in the early 20th century. Dr Syn was a composite figure built up from a number of different real life smugglers active on the marshes in the 18th and 19th centuries, though Thorndike added a clever twist to the character which I won't spoil for you - it is better to buy the books and discover for yourself.

Dymchurch itself lies further along the A259, and is still on the coast. The New Hall, so called because it replaced the Old Hall when built in 1590, was for many years the base for the Lords of the Levels. These "Lords" were local men appointed by the monarch to collect taxes

48

and enforce law and order on the marshes. Their position was abolished in 1866 when their duties were handed over to the Kent county authorities. The old lock-up that they used for incarcerating criminals still exists and is open to the public.

A reminder of the old smuggling days is to be found at the 16th century Ship Inn on the A259 where it forms Dymchurch's High Street. In 1988 renovation work at the inn revealed a small room behind a tiny door in the lounge bar. The room gave access to a hidden passage that snaked off through the thick interior walls of the hotel, apparently providing a secret link between several different rooms. No doubt it was of great use to the smugglers attempting to evade the revenue men. The small room, but not the passageway, is now open and contains a realistic waxwork smuggler together with contraband.

Dymchurch is a stop on the Romney, Hythe and Dymchurch Light Railway. This is a fully-functioning steam railway running on a narrow gauge line from Hythe all the way to the nuclear power station at

49

The monument at Brenzett Aeronautical Museum commemorates those who served here when this was an RAF station during the Battle of Britain.

Dungeness. The nine steam locomotives are small replicas of famous engines that once worked the mainlines of Britain. It was established by Captain Jack Howey, a railway enthusiast, in 1927. During World War II artillery and anti-aircraft guns were mounted on the wagons and hauled by the locomotives to wherever they were needed. The ride is hugely entertaining and if you have time you should go on it. The trains run every day in the summer and on weekends in the winter. On weekdays in winter the trains run to coincide with school opening times.

At the northern end of Dymchurch turn left off the A259 along the lane signposted to Burmarsh. You will find the Lathe Barn Tea Rooms on Donkey Street, the lane heading north to West Hythe. They were closed when I called, but I have it on a personal recommendation that they serve a fine afternoon tea.

Lathe Barn, Tearooms/restaurant, children's farm, craft shops and gift shop. Open March - September, Tuesday to Sunday inclusive. Closed Mondays except bank holidays. Winter season: October, November, February and March, traditional Sunday lunches 12.00 noon - 2.00pm. Wednesday winter warmers 12.00 noon - 1.30pm. www.lathebarn.co.uk

East Guldeford church was built by a local landowner as the marshes were drained to allow his workers to worship without the need to walk miles to an existing church.

The Upper Medway

Start: The Crown, East Street, Turners Hill, Crawley, West Sussex RH10 4PT. Tel: 01342 715218

Finish: Broadview Tea Rooms, Hadlow College, Tonbridge Road, Hadlow, Kent TN11 0AL. Tel: 0500 551434

This drive starts by the headwaters of the Medway River, the largest waterway in Kent. The river rises just over the border in Sussex, so the drive starts there, but most of the route lies in Kent.

Find The Crown at the crossroads in the centre of Turner's Hill. This village, and the hill for which it is named, forms the watershed between those rivers that flow north into the Thames and Thames estuary and those that flow south to the English Channel. Only a mile south of here is a spring that feeds a stream that flows via Ardingly into the Ouse, one of the larger rivers in Sussex that enters the sea at Newhaven. **To find the headwaters of the Medway, leave Turner's Hill driving south on the B2028. Just before the final house, the road passes a pond on the right out of which flows a tiny stream that passes through a culvert under the road then heads off east. This is the nascent Medway, known here as Kent Water.**

Continue south to Selsfield Common. Turn left, then bear immediately left along the lane to Saint Hill. At Saint Hill turn left on the B2110 to East Grinstead. At East Grinstead join the A22 heading south towards Eastbourne. At Forest Row, turn left along the B2110 to drive along the Medway Valley through Upper Hartfield and Hartfield to Withyam and so to Groombridge.

Groombridge was rebuilt by a benevolent landowner in 1623, and a good deal of that model village remains. The most striking building is the church, but several of the tile-hung cottages around the green are just as old. The village was home to the Victorian novelist William Hale White

The former Groombridge Railway Station, now an office complex. The railway is now in the hands of steam enthusiasts who run steam engine services on various days of the year.

who was married in the church here in 1911, and buried here after his sudden death in 1913. White is generally better known by his pen name of Mark Rutherford.

The village is also a terminal for the Spa Valley Railway, a private railway run by enthusiasts that operates steam trains along a line that runs from here to Tunbridge Wells. The steam trains run on weekends, not January or February, and on some weekdays during the summer. See www.spavalleyrailway.co.uk for details.

Groombridge Place lies just off the B2110 half a mile north of the village. The magnificent gardens are open from March to November. Not only are there extensive formal gardens, but the Enchanted Forest is a wide ranging complex of playgrounds, adventure equipment and gardens that are popular with children.

From Groombridge continue along the B2110 to the junction with the A264. Cross straight over the A264 to enter the B2188.

Just past Fordcombe the road crosses the Medway, now a rather more substantial stream. At Penshurst turn right on the B2176 and recross the Medway. After passing through Bidborough the B2176 joins the A26. Turn left and follow the signs for the A26 Maidstone through several roundabouts to the roundabout where A26 turns sharp left and the route straight on is the B2017. Follow the B2017 to Tudeley Green.

The town of Tonbridge is not included in this drive as a stop here would probably consume too much time for an afternoon. However, it is a charming place so you may care to make this drive a full day which would allow ample time to visit the town.

The town originated as a Roman settlement that was taken over by the English when they invaded in the 5th century. This was the highest point that the shallow-draught ships of the day could reach from the sea, which probably accounts for the early prosperity of the place. As ships got larger, Tonbridge lost its seaborne trade but gained it again when the river was canalised this far in the 18th century.

53

The charming row of cottages that overlooks the green at Groombridge.

Further trade came to the town because of the bridge here, for many years the first bridge upstream of that at Rochester. The bridge was guarded by an earth and timber fortification built by the English in the 9th century as a bastion against the Vikings. This was replaced by the Normans with a castle, the massive remains of which dominate the centre of the town to this day. The keep and curtain walls are mostly of Norman work, but the huge gatehouse with its massive drum towers was added in the 14th century. The castle remained intact until the 1640s when it was 'slighted' by Parliamentarian forces to stop it being used by Royalists.

The Church of St Peter and St Paul is likewise of Norman and medieval date, though unlike the castle it is still intact. In Victorian times the church was much enlarged and restored. Not everyone favours the Victorian work, but at least it saved the building from demolition. Also much rebuilt in Victorian times is Tonbridge School, a public school

The gardens at Groombridge Place are filled with all sorts of unexpected surprises, such as these figures formed out of growing wicker.

administered by the Skinners Company of the City of London. The school originated in a trust fund established by merchant Sir Andrew Judd in 1553, but most of the original buildings have not survived.

Just before the bridge at Tudeley the B road turns sharp right and a lane exits to the left. Turn left along this lane to Golden Green. This lane crosses the now extensive flood plain of the Medway. The meadows are criss-crossed by a number of streams which are periodically full or dry depending on how much

The great gatehouse of Tonbridge castle opens off the town centre car park and gives access to the remains of the castle.

55

water is flowing down the valley. The main channel of the Medway is never dry, and is crossed by a bridge.

At Golden Green turn right then left, effectively going straight on, to continue along the lane to Hadlow. At the junction with the A26 turn left to find Hadlow College Tea Rooms on the right as you leave the village adjacent to a garden centre. The tearooms close early on a Sunday, usually around 3.30pm, but otherwise are open to 5pm.

Broadview Tearoom, based within the

Broadview Tearoom

Broadview complex at Hadlow College, uses locally-sourced ingredients to produce a variety of delicious home-made cakes, snacks and soups. Open between 9.00am and 5.00pm Monday to Saturday, and Sunday 10.00am - 4.00pm it possesses a warm and welcoming environment overlooking ten acres of beautiful landscaped gardens.

The King Ethelbert Inn at Reculver stands adjacent to the car park that serves visitors to the nearby Roman fort and Saxon monastery.

The Vanished Wantsum

Start: King Ethelbert Inn, Reculver Lane, Reculver,
Herne Bay, Kent CT6 6SU. Tel: 01227 374368

Finish: The Little Cottage Tea Room, The Quay,
Sandwich, Kent CT13 9EN. Tel: 01304 614387

Today the Wantsum is the name given to a thin, straggly stream that meanders across open farmland from the village of Sarre to the beach just east of Reculver. It must be said that it is a very uninspiring trickle of water. Most drivers hurrying along the A299 between Ramsgate and Herne Bay pass over it without a glance, indeed without knowing it is there.

The Wantsum was not always so insignificant. Indeed, there was a time when the Wantsum was the name given to a stretch of open sea over a mile wide which separated the Isle of Thanet from the mainland. In those days it ran from what is now Cliffs End, just west of Ramsgate northwest to the open beaches east of Reculver.

In Roman times the Wantsum was over a mile wide, and was deep enough to allow free passage to the warships and merchant ships of the time. It proved to be a vital waterway for the Roman fleet both during the invasion of Britain in AD43 and when the Romans were seeking to defend the province of Britain against raiders from northern Germany in the 4th and 5th centuries. At that time the River Soar flowed into the Wantsum between the two little villages aptly named East Stourmouth and West Stourmouth.

The Wantsum seems to have started to disappear around the year 1000 as a combination of falling sea levels, heavy silting and drainage schemes took their toll. By 1400 the northern end of the Wantsum had been closed, but the southern end was still over half a mile wide. This formed an inlet of the sea that reached as far inland as the two Stourmouths. The port of Sandwich, now some two miles inland, was then on the mainland side of the channel. By 1600 Sandwich stood at the head of the inlet, now little more than the estuary of the Soar and its importance as a port was on the wane. By 1750 the coastline was more or less as it is now. The extensive marshes that filled what had been the Wantsum remained treacherous and difficult to negotiate well into the 19th century. Only once they had been drained did the island of Thanet lose its watery boundaries.

This drive starts at Reculver, meanders around and across what was once the Wantsum Channel and ends at Sandwich.

Reculver lies off the A299 east of Herne Bay and is signposted up a lane off the main road. Find the King Ethelbert Inn right at the end of the lane overlooking the sea.

The village of Reculver is now dominated by the great twin towers known as the Two Sisters. These have for centuries served as a vital landmark for sailors in the Thames Estuary. These towers date to the 12th century when the old monastery here was rebuilt. The towers are mostly composed of bricks looted from the Roman ruins and testify to the ancient origins of the site.

Exactly how old Reculver is nobody really knows. In AD43 it was used by the Romans as a port for the merchant ships bringing over supplies for the invasion army that had landed at Richborough and was heading inland. Reculver was then a sheltered bay on the mainland at the northern end of the Wantsum Channel. Whether or not there was a British settlement here before the Romans came is unknown, but likely. Whether there was a native settlement here or not, the Romans built a port and named it Regulbium.

There was probably always a military presence of some sort at Reculver, but it was not until 230 that a fortress was built to guard the harbour. The fort was built on a square design with rounded corners. The walls were of brick and stone, backed by an earthen mound that gave it extra strength and minimal cost. At the corners and intervals along the walls there were stone-built platforms large enough to hold a catapult or other stone-throwing device. There were three gates, in the north, south and east walls. At the centre of the fort was a large brick building that served

59

The great towers of Reculver monastery dominate the coastline of north Kent and have for centuries served as landmarks to sailors entering the Thames estuary.

as a headquarters staff office and a residence for the chief officer on site. Barracks and storerooms of wood filled the rest of the interior of the fort.

The threat that this fortress was designed to face was that of Germanic raiders coming over the North Sea to attack and pillage coastal towns and villages. The variation on this pattern was for the raiders to land near a town and extort blackmail money in return for not attacking. At this date the raiders were not a major problem for the Roman Empire, being more of a nuisance than anything else. They were met by erecting walls around towns close to the coast and having a large number of warships patrolling the main routes used by the raiders. Those warships needed safe bases from which to operate, of which Reculver was one.

In 669 King Egbert of Kent founded a monastery at Reculver. He gave the monks the old Roman fort as a site for their monastery, plus an estate of farming land nearby. The monks renovated the old Roman buildings that were in reasonable condition, and plundered the rest for building stone and bricks for their new buildings. The monastery suffered from Viking raids, but it was a generous new endowment in the 12th century that led to the ancient Roman and old English structures being swept away. In the 12th century the monastery was completely rebuilt in Norman style - with the old Roman fortifications again being used as a source of bricks and stone. The twin towers that dominate the site today date from this rebuilding. They originally were topped by slender spires, but these collapsed after the disestablishment of the monastery under King Henry VIII in the 16th century.

When the Wantsum Channel closed up it altered the coastal currents around this area of Thanet. At Reculver the new set of tidal currents began to erode the soft soil and rocks of the coast. By 1809 the northern sections of the Roman walls had fallen into the sea and the monastic ruins were clearly going to follow before long. That was when the Royal Navy stepped in. The twin towers were such an essential landmark for sailors trying to get up the Thames that they could not be allowed to collapse. The coastline around the towers and fort was strengthened so that the erosion halted. The towers and fortress ruins remain, though they are becoming increasingly isolated as coastal erosion continues nearby.

60

From Reculver drive along the lane back toward the A299. About halfway to the main road, bear left along a lane. Where this lane meets the A299 the main road is a dual carriageway. Just before the lane becomes a slipway onto the main road heading east, turn right along a lane that crosses over the main road and then continue along this lane to Marshside. As the name of this village suggests, it stands on a small rise of ground that marks the mainland shore of the old Wantsum. To the east are the Chislet Marshes which were once part of the Wantsum, but are now drained to form pasture land. **At the far end of Marshside, turn left towards Chislet. Pass through Chislet and then turn left again to Upstreet and a junction with the A28. Turn left. After only about 100 yards turn right down a lane to Grove. As you enter Grove turn left to Preston and then left again to East Stourmouth. Just after passing through this village you will cross the River Stour.** The river originally entered the sea at Stourmouth, but now turns east to flow along what was once the Wantsum Channel toward the sea. **About a mile after crossing the Stour, turn right along the A253 towards Ramsgate, then at a roundabout turn right along the A299, again towards Ramsgate. Just before entering Ramsgate, turn right along the A256 and recross the River Stour. At a roundabout turn right along the lane signposted to Richborough Roman Fort.**

In Roman times, Richborough stood on a peninsula that jutted out into the Wantsum Channel at its southern end. A large harbour sheltered behind this peninsula. It was here that the Roman army first landed when invading Britain in AD43. Once southern Britain had been conquered, the Romans erected a massive triumphal arch on the site to serve as a gateway to the docks of Richborough, and as a permanent reminder of who was in charge. Only the foundations remain, but they remain impressive due to their sheer size.

For two centuries the port here was undefended, though it retained a strong military presence with barracks and constant passage of military men and supplies. When the Germanic raids began, Richborough acquired some ditches and other defences. This would have been at about the time that Reculver was fortified. Then, in around AD275 the entire site was levelled and redeveloped as a specially-constructed fortified naval base and military port. The new defensive walls were 12 feet thick and built of stone bonded with brick. The fort was built on a rectangular plan with huge bastions in the corners and rounded towers projecting at intervals from the walls . The entire fort was surrounded by a double ditch system, probably filled with seawater from the Wantsum.

61

The fort is mentioned in many Roman documents and was clearly a key position in the defences of Britain and Gaul in the later Empire. For historians the excavations here have been important for two main reasons. First the remains of a timber building erected inside the walls in about AD380 showed unmistakably that it had been built as a Christian church, the oldest such structure known in Britain. Secondly the digs turned up a number of Roman coins dating to after the year AD410. This shows that the inhabitants of Roman Britain remained in touch with the collapsing imperial domains long after the emperors

The mighty walls of Richborough Roman Fort, one of the string of coastal forts in souther Britain that together made up the static defences of the Saxon Shore.

granted Britain its independence and told the province to look after its own defence. It also shows that the Romano-British authorities who held power here after AD410 continued to use and maintain the Roman military structures for some years, probably for several decades.

After visiting Richborough, return to the A256 and cross over to enter the lane signposted to Sandwich. If Richborough was the main port on the Wantsum in Roman times, that role had been taken over by Sandwich by around AD750. The town is one of the most delightful in England with dozens of medieval houses, shops and other buildings crowding along the old medieval street plan that has not altered in more than a thousand years.

Parking in the town itself is a bit difficult given the narrow streets, but there are spacious car parks outside the old town walls. Each car park has a map of the town to help you get your bearings before plunging into the maze of alleys and streets. The Little Cottage Tea Room stands on The Quay, one of the easier streets to locate in Sandwich. This street was the old dockside area and still looks out over a small marina used by yachts and other small craft that come up the Soar from the sea. The Little Cottage is closed on most Mondays, but is open on Bank Holiday Mondays. They serve light lunches as well as morning coffee, afternoon tea and a range of cakes and pastries.

Among the buildings worth seeking out is the Fisher Gate, the massive medieval structure that guards the entrance to the town from The Quay. A short walk to the north stands the even larger Barbican Gate, built to mount more up-to-date artillery by King Henry VIII in 1539. These military installations are a reminder that a major port like Sandwich would have been a valuable strategic prize in times of war.

In fact there are no fewer than seven recorded Battles of Sandwich. The first occurred in 850 when King Athelstan of England attacked a force of Vikings who had landed here and captured the town. Nine of the Viking ships were captured and hundreds of the invaders killed before they fled out to sea. In 991 the Vikings were back under the Danish king Swein Forkbeard. This time they came with 93 ships, each carrying around 40 men, to plunder and burn the town. In 1009 it was an English civil war that led to a naval battle just off the entrance to the port. Little is known about this battle, we don't even know why the rebel nobleman Wulfnoth had rebelled against King Ethelred the Unready. Whatever the cause of the violence, Wulfnoth won the battle and chased the surviving ships of the royal fleet up the Wantsum and as far as London Bridge. In 1048 a Viking fleet of unknown size was defeated by an English fleet off the port.

63

In 1217 a pirate fleet led by a Frenchman known as Eustace the Monk tried to capture Sandwich as the opening move in a campaign to plunder his way around the English coast. He was ambushed in the entrance to the Wantsum by a fleet led by Hubert de Burgh, who wasted little time in boarding the French flagship. Eustace was killed and his head hoisted on a pike, whereupon the remaining French ships fled. Another French attack in 1457 led to a battle outside the city walls in which the then Mayor of Sandwich was killed leading his troops. The mayors have ever since worn a black robe as a mark of mourning.

In 1460 Sandwich saw a pivotal action in the opening stages of the Wars of the Roses. For years the recurrent madness of King Henry VI had allowed his avaricious wife, Margaret, and her cronies to plunder the royal finances and plunge England into an era of corrupt and inefficient government that, among other things, saw the loss of all the hereditary English lands in France except for the fortified port of Calais. The queen had been opposed by Richard, Duke of York. York was the king's cousin, a famously able and honest man. The conflict had come to a head early in 1460 when Henry formally adopted York as his heir and put the reins of government into his hands.

Margaret responded by raising an army and putting it under the command of the Duke of Somerset with orders to kill York. Somerset caught York and his bodyguard at Wakefield. Despite a gallant last stand, the outnumbered Yorkists were heavily defeated. Both York and his eldest son were killed. Hearing the news, York's two other sons, Edward and Richard, fled abroad. Richard was only a boy so he went to live with foreign relatives, but Edward was a young man of fighting age. He went to Calais to beg for help from the governor there, his cousin the Earl of Warwick. Warwick gave Edward shelter while he sent men to England to gauge how much support Margaret had for her murderous policies.

Margaret, meanwhile, sent one of her chief supporters, Sir Richard Woodville, to gather a fleet at Sandwich to transport an army to Calais. She hoped to intimidate Warwick into handing over Edward, who could then be quietly killed. Warwick, however, had by this time got reports that England was restive under Margaret's corrupt and violent rule. He struck first.

Just before dawn a fleet of German merchant ships put into Sandwich. Nothing unusual there, except that these ships had been hired by Warwick and were packed with armed men. Warwick led the assault himself, aided by several Sandwich men who had crossed to Calais a few days earlier. Surprise was so complete that Woodville was asleep when the Yorkists burst into his room. Still dressed in their nightclothes, Woodville and his family were hustled off to be locked below in the ships. Warwick quickly captured the fleet being prepared to attack Calais and less than an hour after landing was back at sea and heading home.

65

Just one of the dozens of medieval and Tudor houses that are crammed into the ancient walled city of Sandwich, one of the most historic in Kent.

The raid was short, but had massive political impact. Margaret could now not kill young Edward, and once that was known all those unhappy with her rule began preparing themselves to support Edward when he returned. Edward landed in 1461 and in a lightning campaign lasting less than three months utterly defeated Margaret and her allies. Henry VI was persuaded to abdicate and put into comfortable quarters under armed guard. He would later be murdered when Margaret tried to raise a fresh rebellion in 1470.

The ancient medieval churches of Sandwich are well worth visiting. Not only do they have stunning architecture - one of them has the largest wooden roof in Kent - but they have a mass of memorials and sculpture to view.

When you have finished looking around the town, its museums and monuments, you might care to enjoy the tasty snack of the same name as the town. The sandwich was named for John Montague, 4th Earl of Sandwich, who rose high in the government of Britain in the 1770s, but who proved to be utterly incompetent. Sandwich's main problem was that he preferred gambling and drinking to working in his office. So dedicated to gambling was he that he resented leaving the card tables to eat a meal. He therefore came up with the idea of slapping a slice of meat between two slices of bread. This enabled him to eat while gaming, but without getting his hand messy and so affecting the cards. The 'sandwich' was born. It is worth having one while in Sandwich.

Supernatural Swale

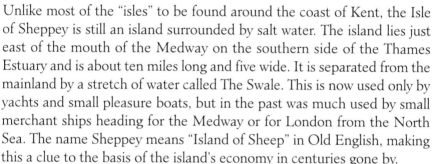

Start: The Aviator, Queenborough Corner, Queenborough, Sheerness, Kent, ME12 3DJ. Tel: 01795 666094

Finish: Oad Street Tea Room, Oad Street, Borden, Kent ME9 8LB. Tel: 01795 844182

Unlike most of the "isles" to be found around the coast of Kent, the Isle of Sheppey is still an island surrounded by salt water. The island lies just east of the mouth of the Medway on the southern side of the Thames Estuary and is about ten miles long and five wide. It is separated from the mainland by a stretch of water called The Swale. This is now used only by yachts and small pleasure boats, but in the past was much used by small merchant ships heading for the Medway or for London from the North Sea. The name Sheppey means "Island of Sheep" in Old English, making this a clue to the basis of the island's economy in centuries gone by.

Strictly speaking Sheppey should be called the Isles of Sheppey as there were originally three islands here. The largest was Sheppey itself, but the islands of Harty and Elmley once stood off its southern shore. Both of these smaller islands have now been joined to Sheppey as the tidal flats and marshes that separated them have been drained and reclaimed.

The island can be approached only by the Kingsferry Bridge that carries the A249 across The Swale north of Sittingbourne. Find The Aviator at the junction of the A249 and A250.

Leaving the pub, drive northeast along the A250 to the junction with the B2008. Take the B2008 east for about 4 miles, then turn left along the lane signposted to Warden Point. The coast here is eroding fairly rapidly and you will eventually find the lane is blocked off to traffic. If you continue on foot you will come to the spot where the road ends abruptly in a cliff. The wreckage of the parts of the road that used to continue on to the east can be seen on the beach below and scattered over the face of the cliff.

The first of the ghosts and spooks to be encountered on this drive roams the fields and shoreline around Warden. This is the ghost of Sir John Sawbridge who lived in Warden Manor in the 17th century. He was widely rumoured to have led the gang conducting the smuggling which was then prevalent in the area. He was never caught, but justice caught up with him in grisly form. He was riding out late one night - allegedly to inspect an incoming cargo of smuggled French brandy - when his horse bolted and he was thrown. Sawbridge was badly injured, and was not found until well past dawn, by which time his injuries had become fatal. He died later that day. Ever since, his angry ghost has been seen riding around this area on a terrifyingly large black stallion.

Drive south through Warden to Leysdown-on-Sea. Turn right along the B2231 towards Eastchurch. Turn left up a lane to the Isle of Harty. This road winds over a hill before dropping down to cross flat levels and a tidal stream named the Capel Fleet. This is all that is left of the tidal flats that once separated Harty from Sheppey. In the days before the marshes and tidal flows were drained this was a lonely, eerie place. When the chill wind blew through the reeds and dank vegetation the area seemed almost other worldly. Perhaps that is how the place got its name. In Old English, the name derives from a phrase which, in modern parlance, might be loosely rendered as "The Marsh of Monsters".

Intriguingly, the name is fairly close to the name Heorot, the great hall plagued by a man-eating monster in the ancient English poem Beowulf. The topography of the Heorot in the poem closely matches that of the area around Harty. The cliffs on the east coast of Sheppey shine when wet, as do those in the poem, and it is possible to ride a horse down them - though only just. Other similarities are numerous, and the history of this region makes it likely that Harty was an off-shore English stronghold off a Romano-British mainland about the time the poem was composed.

It is an intriguing possibility that the Marsh of Monsters in this isolated area of Kent might have been the inspiration for the most ancient literature in the English language. Whatever the truth of this, the monsters have not been seen since the marshes were drained some generations ago.

Having viewed what remains of the Marsh of Monsters, return along the lane to the B2231 and turn left. Pass through Eastchurch to reach the A249. Turn left and leave Sheppey over the Kingsferry Bridge. At the junction with the A2 turn right and drive through Newington and into Rainham. In Rainham you need to park and make your way to the church. On the stroke of midnight, on nights of a full moon, a black coach materialises slowly outside the gates of the Church of St Helen and St Giles. The coach is driven by a tall man dressed in a voluminous dark cloak, but nobody can tell you what his face is like for he is headless. Also headless are

The church at Rainham is said to be the haunt of the most dramatic and terrifying phantom in Kent - perhaps of all England.

the four jet black stallions which pull the coach. For a few seconds the coach waits, then the figure of a man comes out of the church and walks down the path to the gate. Climbing into the ghastly coach, the man calmly removes his head from his shoulders and holds it in his lap.

Then they are off. The coachman lashes the horses with a whip that cracks as loud as thunder. Breaking into an instant gallop, the horses pull the coach at breakneck speed. Sparks as bright as lightning flash from the horses' hooves as they strike the road. Anyone foolish enough not to get out of the way is blown aside as if struck by an enormously powerful blast of wind. The air is as hot as a furnace or, more likely, as hot as hell.

This startling manifestation is said to be the coach, attendants and eternally damned spirit of Bad Squire Bloor. Known more properly as Sir Christopher Bloor, this notorious debauchee was the local landowner in the later 16th century. He was infamous for his drunken and riotous lifestyle – which involved the seduction and desertion of local maidens too numerous to mention as well as brawls and punch-ups. The centre of the outrageous events was Bloors Place, where Sir Christopher would throw wild parties for his drinking partners from London, Canterbury and other cities. Women of easy virtue were always invited to sate the desires of the Bad Squire and his mates. Or Sir Christopher would set out in his coach to tour the taverns of the area, picking fights and smashing furniture.

When Sir Christopher was found dead in the road outside Bloors Place one morning after a particularly wild night out it was rumoured that he had been murdered by the father of one of the maids he had ruined. But the fact that there was not a mark on his body led to another story - that the Devil had come to Rainham to collect his own.

70

The desolate marshes that separate the Isle of Harty from the Isle of Sheppey. The name for this area derives from an Old English term for water monsters.

Leave Rainham heading east along the A2 to pass back through Newington, then through Sittingbourne to reach Faversham, which lies just north of the main road. Parking in the town centre is restricted, but there is a large car park which also features a town map to help you find your way about. The first haunted site to visit is the Fleur-de-Lis Heritage Centre which houses the Faversham Society and the local museum. This is haunted by a lady in a long white dress. She is seen most often at the top of the stairs and along the upstairs corridor. Staff in the museum have also reported that the antique telephone exchange on display will suddenly ring, though it has not been connected to any lines for years.

The Guildhall is also haunted, this time by a ghost that is heard rather than seen. The centre of the disturbances are in the committee room where footsteps have been heard walking about when nobody has been moving. The footsteps are also heard in the council chamber. Rather less often, the sound of a female voice calling out from empty rooms may be heard.

71

Faversham's most famous ghost is to be found not in the town centre itself, but at the Shipwrights Arms pub which lies beside a tidal creek on the lane toward Oare. Late one stormy night in the early 19th century a sailor was found slumped a few yards from the door of the pub. His footsteps led back to the muddy foreshore and The Swale beyond. The weather was dreadful, but none of those who braved the elements could see any vessel in the sheltered waters. The sailor himself died soon afterwards without recovering his senses and next day wreckage was washed up to show that some small vessel had foundered the night before. No other survivors were found so where the ship had come from remained a mystery.

It was surmised that the sailor had somehow got ashore from the stricken vessel and had made his way towards the welcoming lights of the pub before collapsing from exhaustion.

It would seem that the ghost is now recreating his failed mission to summon help for his stricken ship. He comes up from the creek, staggering over the mud flats, on dark and blustery winter nights. As the ghost approaches the pub his step becomes firmer and stance more upright. As he reaches the front door, the ghost pushes it open and strides in. Then he vanishes as if a light had been switched off.

Witnesses describe the sailor as being a tall, broad man dressed in an old-fashioned and dark-coloured reefer jacket. His hair is long and dark, tied back into a plait or ponytail. With him he brings a strong stench of tobacco and rum, which is only right considering his profession. His eyes are red and wide, and it is these that seem to be his most noticeable feature. Some describe how he glares at them, others that he stares sightless in front of him, still more that his eyes look as if he has been weeping.

Who the phantom sailor was and where he came from will never be known. But he must have cared deeply for those whom he left behind on his doomed ship for his endless mission to save them continues generations after he first failed in the attempt.

Return along the A2 and pass through Sittingbourne. Turn left along the A249. Just past the junction with the M2, turn off the main road along the lane signposted to Oad Street and Borden. Find Oad Street Tea Room just as you enter the hamlet of Oad Street. They are open 9am to 5pm, seven days a week and offer a hearty range of traditional English foods at lunch time as well as wonderful afternoon teas.

Oad Street Centre has developed from a small craft shop into a thriving business, which houses an outstanding tea room/restaurant, a unique

gift shop and a stunning art gallery. The centre is also home to three workshops, picture framers, a pottery and a furniture restorer. Admission to the centre is free and is open seven days a week 9.30am - 5.30pm including bank holidays.

Faversham's Shipwrights Arms pub stands a mile or so out of town on the edge of the tidal creeks that dominate this coast. It is haunted by a sailor who died in a shipping tragedy over a century ago.

Windmill Hills

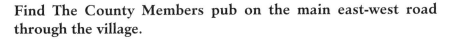

Start: The County Members, Aldington Road, Lympne, Hythe, Kent CT21 4LH. Tel: 01303 264759

Finish: The Village Tea Rooms, 31-33, High Street, Headcorn, Kent TN27 9NE. Tel: 01622 890682

Find The County Members pub on the main east-west road through the village.

In Roman times Lympne stood on the coast. The extensive flat lands that are now the productive grazing grounds for sheep of Romney Marsh to the south were then shallow seawater with an island, now Lydd, some miles to the southwest. See Drive 7 Smugglers Marsh for details of how the coastline has altered over the centuries. The Romans knew this village as Portus Lemanis and used it as a small commercial harbour. The River Rother ran into the sea not far from here in those distant days, though it now enters the sea far to the southwest at Rye.

In the later 3rd century a fort was built to protect the harbour. The stone and brick walls were massively thick - up to 14 feet - and stood over 20 feet tall. This was one of the later forts to be built by the Romans to defend what they termed the Saxon Shore, the coastline most often raided by Saxon and Frankish warriors crossing the North Sea from northern Germany. The complex system of defences was formed of a string of coastal forts stretching from the Humber to the Isle of Wight in Britain and from the mouth of the Rhine to the Seine in Gaul. As well as the forts and the soldiers who manned them, the defences included a large fleet of warships intended to intercept the raiders at sea.

The fort at Lympne was one of the last to be constructed, being begun in around 320. Unlike most other Roman forts it was not laid out in rectangular plan, but follows an irregular polygonal shape. This was probably due to the fact that the fort had to be squeezed onto an irregular peninsula of land between the harbour and the sea. Over the

The County Members at Lympne takes its name from the gentlemen that Kent has sent to represent the county in Parliament in the days when the county elected a number of MPs jointly rather than being divided up into individual constituencies.

centuries, the sea and marsh have retreated, advanced and retreated again. The damp, soft soil has not proved equal to the task of supporting the heavy stone walls, most of which have toppled over. The ruins are now fragmentary, but still worth investigating. They can be found on the hillside that drops down behind the church, a public footpath giving access to the Roman fort.

Standing on the hill above the Roman fort is the medieval Lympne Castle. This was begun as a wooden edifice soon after the Norman Conquest. It was built around the old Roman watchtower from which lookouts formerly kept a watch for German raiders trying to get through the Dover Straits to reach vulnerable coasts to the west. The wooden castle was torn down in 1360 and rebuilt in stone, at which time the Roman tower was remodelled to become the great square keep that dominates the scene today. The castle was restored in 1905 and remains a private home.

From Lympne head west along the B2067. This road has a low ridge to its north and the vast flat expanses of Romney Marsh to the south. In Roman times this was very roughly the line of the coast. In later centuries, as the marshes began to form, the River Rother meandered across the flat lands. **Just beyond the village of Hamstreet go straight across the A2070 and continue along the B2067 to Woodchurch. At Woodchurch turn right into the village, almost at once bearing left at a Y-junction.** This lane passes the church, when you should see the windmill on top of the hill to the right.

Windmills were once a common feature of the English landscape. A form of windmill was developed in what is now Iran in around AD700, but this worked on a vertical shaft principle and was quite different from the more familiar form with a horizontal shaft and vertical sails. This form of windmill seems to have been developed in northwestern Europe in the 12th century. The earliest certain reference dates to 1191 when a windmill at Bury St Edmunds featured in a legal dispute. However, windmills were so widely spread across southern England and the Low Countries within a few years that it seems certain they had been invented at least as early as 1150.

75

These early windmills were of the post variety in which the whole structure is mounted on a stout wooden post and turned to face the wind. In around 1270, the tower windmill was developed. This had a round stone tower as its main structure. The sails were mounted on a wooden cap, which was alone turned to face the wind. This more robust structure meant that larger windmills with bigger sails could be built, in turn making the amount of power that could be captured much greater.

Throughout the medieval period, mills continued to be powered by water if a

The fine cream tea served at The Village Tea Rooms in the High Street of Headcorn.

The village sign for Lympne incorporates castle, church and the old Roman name for the fortress that lies at the foot of the hill.

76

fast-flowing stream was nearby, or by wind if not. A sudden ridge such as that by Lympne was ideal for a windmill. The flat marshes to the south provided no obstacle to the wind which swept in off the sea to power the windmills.

Return to the B2067 and continue heading west to Tenterden, perhaps one of the most charming towns in southern England. The High Street is composed mostly of Georgian shops and houses, many of them built of wooden weatherboarding, though there are a few Tudor houses as well. **Leave Tenterden heading south on the A28 towards Hastings. After about three miles turn right on to the B2086 towards Hartley. At Hartley turn right on the A229 to reach Cranbrook. At Cranbrook turn right into the village centre, then at the church turn along the lane to Golford and find the Union Mill on your left as you leave the village.**

The mill was built in 1814 and, at 72 feet tall, is the second tallest mill in the country. At first the mill ground local grain into flour for local bakers and families to purchase. That trade had flourished ever since windmills had been invented but by the mid-19th century it was fading as cheaper grain was being brought in from North America and Australia, to be ground at steam-powered mills on the dockside. By 1870

The hill on which Lympne Castle is built offers stunning views across Romney Marsh, with distant Dungeness Power Station being visible on a clear day.

the Union Mill had abandoned wind power and was using a small steam engine instead. Likewise the flour trade had largely gone, so the mill was grinding coarse grain and meal for animal food.

The Mill has now been restored to its former glory and is once again a fully-functioning windmill grinding grain into flour. Bags of the flour, available in various grades, can be purchased in the on-site shop. There are fully-guided tours around the mill so that visitors can see the various stages of milling and the machinery of a bygone age. The mill is open most Saturdays from April to September, and on various other days as well. See www.unionmill.org.uk/ for details.

Leave Cranbrook on the A229 heading north to Staplehurst. At the roundabout with the A262 turn right towards Biddenden. This is a pretty village with a green, nearly all the houses on which have been listed, along with most of the buildings in the High Street. Many of these are 16th century weavers' workshops.

Woodchurch windmill stands on a hill above the village. It is open to the public on summer Sundays.

The fame of Biddenden rests on the Biddenden Maids. These were two sisters named Chulkhurst who were born here in the 12th century. The girls were one the earliest known examples of conjoined twins, being born joined at the shoulder and hip. They lived happy and contented lives for 34 years. When they died they bequeathed their wealth to the Chulkhurst Trust to provide bread and cheese to the poor of the parish. To this day bread and cheese is distributed on Easter Monday to any pensioners who present themselves. The old almshouses where the ceremony is performed is known, appropriately enough, as the Bread and Cheese House. A sign featuring the Maids dominates the small green.

At Biddenden turn left on the A274 towards Maidstone. After about five miles the road enters Headcorn. Find the Village Tea Rooms on the main road, just before the church. They are open 9.30am to 4.30pm, seven days a week. On Thursdays, Fridays and Saturdays they are open in the evenings as well to serve a good selection of bistro dishes.

The Union Mill lies up a narrow alley on the outskirts of Cranbrook. There is no parking in the lane, so leave your car in the village centre car park.

The old ford at Eynsford is still open to motorised traffic, though after heavy rain it might not be advisable to take the average family car through it. The adjacent medieval packhorse bridge offers a drier alternative for pedestrians and horses.

The Darent Valley

Start: The Bull, 293 London Road, Greenhithe, DA9 9DA. Tel: 01322 382006

Finish: Ellenor Teashop, 11a High Street, Otford, TN14 5PG. Tel: 01959 524322

The Darent was one of the more charming river valleys in southern England. In recent decades its lower reaches have become swallowed up by the sprawling edges of London's suburbs. Since 1965 the section of the river from the confluence with the Cray to the Thames has formed the formal boundary between Kent and Greater London. The once charming little town of Dartford a couple of miles upstream along the Darent from the Thames has become a growing industrial town with congested streets and a mass of factory complexes. Many people think that the Darent Valley must be much the same as Dartford, the name was originally Darentford, but this is very far from the truth as this drive will reveal.

The drive starts at the The Bull which stands on the A226 as it passes through Greenhithe. Leave Greenhithe heading west on the A226 to Dartford. In Dartford turn left along the A225 towards Sevenoaks. After passing under the M20, the A225 crosses the A20 at a roundabout and then enters Eynsford. It is here that the valley leaves the London suburbs behind and enters charming, gentle Kent countryside. Eynsford itself is a charming little village of half-timbered cottages with some modern building. As the name of the village would suggest, there is a ford over the Darent here. There is also an old packhorse bridge over the river alongside the ford, both of which are still in use.

Since about 1150 the village has been dominated by Eynsford Castle, built by Sir William D'Eynsford who was a favoured knight at the court of King Henry II. The construction of the castle and the establishment of Sir William's estates in the area brought the young knight into a

The idyllic village of Eynsford is grouped around the church, ford and pub all of which lie within about 150 yards of each other.

dispute with the see of Canterbury. The details of the dispute have not been preserved, but were involved in the larger question of who had ultimate control over lands owned by the Church in England: King or Pope. Sir William clearly favoured the authority of the king and so sought the permission of King Henry for certain works that intruded on the estates of Canterbury. He obtained from Henry the needed permission and paid to the see of Canterbury the price set.

It was unfortunate for Sir William that the Archbishop of Canterbury at the time was Thomas Becket, an uncompromising supporter of papal rights. He announced that Sir William's actions were illegal as he had not sought permission of the Pope and so began a tortuous series of legal actions. Unsurprisingly, Sir William became one of Becket's most outspoken critics and was loud in his demands that King Henry should put the archbishop, and the Church, firmly in their place. Henry was himself involved in complex and difficult legal actions with Becket, as well as in the more general dispute, and knew that many knights who had taken his side in the dispute were being harassed by Church authorities.

In 1170 Henry heard that Becket had begun a new legal action against yet another knight loyal to the king. Henry lost his temper, rounding on his assembled court with the words "Will no one rid me of this turbulent priest?" Sir William joined the general clamour for action. Unknown to Sir William or King Henry four other knights had taken the king at his word. They rode hard to Canterbury, stormed into the cathedral and hacked Becket to death. Sir William was so appalled by the results of his rash words that he vowed never again to set foot on the disputed lands nor to live at Eynsford Castle. Henry, for his part, was forced to do public penances at Becket's tomb and to give in to the pope on many points.

Sir William's successors were not so delicate as he was and took up residence in the castle. It was not abandoned until the changing military technology rendered its

83

The Uranus pillar of the unique Otford Solar System Monument. This is one of the more distant pillars in the system being almost a mile from the Sun pillar in the recreation ground.

walls obsolete. Today the flint and stone walls stand up to 30 feet tall in places and are well worth a look. The castle stands just off the High Street opposite the aptly named Castle Inn.

The small modern bridge at Otford. This replaced the ancient ford around which raged a battle fought here more than a thousand years ago.

In Eynsford turn off right down the lane signposted to Lullingstone Villa. Bits and pieces of Roman date had been turning up here since the 1750s, but it was not until 1949 that anyone realised that a villa lay here. The complex of buildings was found to be in a magnificent state of preservation, complete with stunning mosaic floors, which enabled archaeologists to trace the development of this home-farm complex from when it was founded in around AD60 to its utter destruction by fire in around AD450. The dates were significant, meaning that it was founded within a generation of the Roman invasion and destroyed during the wars fought as the Roman Empire collapsed. The site is owned by English Heritage and is open to the public every day in the summer months and weekends in January and February.

After viewing the villa, return to the A225 and continue south to Otford. Park in the recreation ground to view the famous Otford Solar System, built in 2000 as a project to mark the Millennium. The monument is a scale model of the real solar system on a scale of about 1:4.5 billion. The Sun is represented by a brass dome mounted on a stone pillar in the recreation ground. The planets Mercury, Venus, Earth and Mars are also

84

marked by pillars in the recreation ground. The more distant planets of Jupiter, Saturn, Neptune, Uranus and Pluto are indicated by pillars elsewhere around the village and are linked by a marked walk - it takes about 45 minutes if you are feeling energetic enough.

While your car is parked in the recreation ground car park, it is worth walking along the lane to the bridge over the Darent. This was the site of a battle in 776 when King Offa of Mercia sent an army to invade Kent and impose Mercian overlordship on King Egbert. The battle was fought here as Egbert sought not only to block the invasion of his kingdom, but also to inflict such a defeat on the Mercians that Offa would think twice before seeking to throw his weight around in Kent again.

It is unfortunate that no account of the actual fighting has survived. We know that both armies were composed overwhelmingly of infantry armed with spear, dagger and shield, the richer men had helmets and swords. We know also that the favoured tactic of the time was the shield wall, in

The historic village centre of Otford clusters around the village green and pond.

which the men formed up shoulder to shoulder and eight or more ranks deep to form a solid phalanx of fighting men. Given that the Darent was then wider than today with marshy banks and lined by trees, this style of massive formation fighting would not have been possible at the ford itself. There is some evidence, though not much, that Egbert lured part of the Mercian host over the ford, then attacked while the enemy were divided. Such a ruse would have allowed the Kentish men to form a shield wall, but in truth we do not really know.

What is certain is that Egbert won his battle, and that he won it in convincing fashion. The Mercian survivors hurried back to the safety of the walled city of London and Offa never again tangled with Egbert. We do not know how long Egbert lived after this momentous battle, but by 784 he had been succeeded by King Elmund, who seems to have been a cousin of some kind. The Mercians were still determined to annex the kingdom of Kent. See Drive 7 Smugglers Marsh for details of the final act in the conflict.

86

Having viewed the battlefield and model solar system, find Ellenor Tea Shop on the High Street about 100 yards east of the bridge and almost opposite the recreation ground. Ellenor's is open 10am to 4.30pm Mondays to Saturdays, but is closed on a Sunday.

Hengist's Footsteps

Start: The Sportsman Inn, 123 Sandwich Road, Cliffs End, Kent CT12 5JB. Tel: 01843 592175

Finish: Mulberry Tea Rooms, 2 Station Road, Birchington, CT7 9DQ. Tel: 01843 846805

The name of Hengist was one to strike terror into the heart of any peace-loving person in the mid-5th century. He was the leader of a notoriously savage band of mercenaries and a military commander of undoubted power and effectiveness. His services were sought by those in power and feared by anyone who crossed his path. It is unfortunate that we do not know more about him than we do. But what we do know is that he was to become the first King of Kent and that he stalked the county from one end to the other. This drive takes in some of the more significant sites in his career. This route is by far the longest drive in this book, but there is no real need to stop at any place for more than a few minutes and everything can be seen from the car.

Hengist lived in the century after the Roman Empire abandoned the province of Britain in 410. This is a time when dates are notoriously difficult to pin down with any certainty. The only really firm date in Hengist's life is that on which he first arrived in Kent: 449. Even that date is not agreed by all historians, some of whom prefer to place it earlier in around 429. I shall follow the traditional dating in this account.

Hengist was born in about 420 somewhere in what is now northern Germany or southern Denmark. He belonged to a Germanic people called the Jutes, closely linked to the Saxons and Angles who inhabited northern Germany. He was not a king, but may have been born into the royal family and was certainly a nobleman. Like most men of his time and place he was trained in the arts of war, and soon excelled in them. He fought a number of campaigns on the continent before he came to the attention of the Romano-British authorities. At this time Britain had been abandoned by Rome but its internal government was still intact

The ship "Hugin" was built in 1949 in Denmark, then rowed over the North Sea by a team of volunteers to recreate the voyage made by the mercenary Hengist when he came from Denmark to Britain, traditionally in the year 449.

and functioning along Roman lines. There was a patchwork of local authorities, each elected by the local men of wealth and influence. These had appointed a senior magistrate to settle disputes between them and to co-ordinate issues that affected the whole province, such as defence. That official was Vortigern.

By the 440s, Vortigern was facing Pictish raiders from across Hadrian's Wall to the north, seaborne pillagers from Ireland and Germans attacking the east coast by sailing across from Germany. To face them he had local troops to man city walls and other local defences. He also had a mobile central army that he could move to face a threat as it developed. He may have had a fleet of sorts based on the old Roman fortified harbours of the Saxon Shore - see Drive 9 The Vanished Wantsum and Drive 11 Windmill Hills for details. At least some of the men under his command were Germanic mercenaries. In 449 Vortigern hired Hengist, who came to Britain with his brother Horsa and three shiploads of tough mercenary fighters.

Find The Sportsman Inn on the A256 about a mile south of the roundabout junction with the A299. In Hengist's time this stood on the very edge of the Isle of Thanet. Stretching south where there are now flat pasture lands was the Wantsum Channel, an arm of the sea more than a mile wide that completely cut off Thanet from the mainland. See Drive 9 The Vanished Wantsum for details of this waterway. From the pub drive north toward Ramsgate to find the magnificent ship "Hugin" standing amid parkland to the right of the road. This is a replica of the type of ship used by Hengist and Horsa to come to Britain. It was rowed over the North Sea by a group of history enthusiasts in 1949 to mark the 1500th anniversary of the voyage by the original mercenaries. After the voyage it was hauled out of the sea and placed here as a memorial.

Hengist was welcomed by Vortigern who gave him the Isle of Thanet to be a base for his men and ships. For the next few years Hengist and Horsa worked hard for the Romano-Britons. They patrolled the east coast in their ships, driving off or destroying raiding parties of Picts or other Germans. Sometime around 455 the British local authorities fell out with each other, apparently over who should pay for the soldiers defending the province. Vortigern led one faction, a nobleman named Ambrosius Aurelianus the other. The quarrel came to blows at Wallop in Hampshire. Vortigern turned to his employee Hengist for help in the dispute.

89

Hengist eagerly agreed. He sent back to Germany for more mercenaries and proposed that the deal be settled by a marriage alliance. He offered his daughter to Vortigern, who accepted. As a price for his help in Vortigern's troubles, Hengist asked for and was given control of all Kent. At the time Kent was a local government area known as Cantium within the post-Roman system. What Hengist seems to have got was the position of chief magistrate within the existing government of Kent.

Leave the Hugin driving south on the A256. After about four miles turn right at a roundabout on the A257 to Canterbury. Drive to the city centre and, if you wish, park. The main sight here linked to Hengist are the city walls. Although these have been patched up, improved and repaired many times over the centuries, they are substantially the Roman walls that stood here when Hengist arrived. With the authority of Vortigern behind him, Hengist had no trouble occupying the city. The existing chief magistrate of Cantium, a man named Gwyrangon, was unimpressed. He fled to Ambrosius nursing his grievances.

For some time, perhaps a few years, a fragile peace existed. Then a dispute broke out between Hengist and Vortigern over unpaid bills. Hengist left Canterbury on the old Roman road to London, now the A2, to extract the money that he was owed by force. **Leave Canterbury on the A2. Drive through Faversham, Sittingbourne, Chatham, Rochester and Gravesend. Pass Dartford on the modern bypass, then turn off on the A223 to Crayford. In Crayford turn right on the A226 to find the bridge over the River Cray.**

A Victorian view of the arrival of Hengist on the Isle of Thanet to be met by the British leader Vortigern. The meeting would prove to be instrumental in turning post-Roman Britain into England.

This was the site of the great battle between the advancing Saxon and Jutish mercenaries led by Hengist and the defending Romano-Britons under Vortigern's son Vortimer. There was no bridge here then, only a ford. The battle ended in a crushing victory for the rebels. Vortimer and his surviving men fled back to London and barricaded themselves within the city walls. Hengist at this point announced that he was now King of Kent. The move threw off any allegiance to the formal post-Roman government of Britain and at the same time made him supreme ruler within Kent, no longer merely the chief magistrate of Cantium.

Hengist and Horsa proceeded to rampage across southern Britain. Other groups of Germanic mercenaries based elsewhere also rose in rebellion to loot, pillage and kill. Lincolnshire went up in flames, so did much of Yorkshire and what is now East Anglia. The undisputed leaders of the uprising were Hengist and Horsa. For the most part the mercenaries were unable to break into heavily defended cities, though some smaller towns fell amid scenes of slaughter. By the time autumn was coming, Hengist and Horsa were back in the newly-founded kingdom of Kent to entrench their power.

Soon afterwards, perhaps the following summer, the Romano-Britons counterattacked. Vortigern led the fighting north of the Thames, his sons Vortimer and Categirn invaded Kent.

Leave Crayford on the A226 heading east. Join the M25 heading south towards Sevenoaks. At the junction with the M20 turn off and head east towards Maidstone. Leave the M20 at junction 6 and go north on the A229, following signs for Aylesford. In Aylesford find the old bridge. The battle fought here ended in a stalemate with both Categirn and Horsa being killed. See Drive 6 The Battle Gap for details of this battle.

Although the Romano-British invasion was halted on this occasion they were soon back. Hengist was soon in full retreat across Kent, being forced to abandon his capital city of Canterbury to the advancing enemy. **Leave Aylesford and return to the M20; leave at junction 8 and join the A20 to Canterbury. Leave Canterbury on the A257 towards Sandwich. At the roundabout junction, turn left along the A256 towards Ramsgate. A lane on the left is signposted to Richborough Roman Fort.** It was here that Hengist turned to fight. According to a triumphant British chronicle that recorded Vortimer's victory "Hengist and the barbarians were beaten and put to flight. They drowned as they clambered aboard their keels like women."

But Hengist did not go far - only as far as Thanet. **Continue north along the A256 to return to the Hugin ship.** Holed up on Thanet, Hengist sent overseas to Germany for more men to come to join him and the other rebels now on the defensive further north. They came in their thousands and the war between Saxon and Briton raged on for some years. Finally, a treaty was agreed that would be signed at a great conference, traditionally held at Stonehenge. At that conference, Hengist proved to be treacherous. He secretly summoned an army which slaughtered the British delegates and captured Vortigern. The British collapsed into civil war, allowing Hengist to retake all of Kent.

Hengist died in about 488. He was buried at some unknown location under a pagan grave mound overlooking the sea. Very likely he was buried on the coast of Thanet. In his career he had established the Jutes and Saxons as permanent settlers in eastern Britain. They would soon be joined by Angles settling in the north. Together the three peoples would eventually come together to become the English and would conquer most of Britain.

Leave the ship Hugin on the A299 heading east. At a junction with the A28 turn right towards Margate. As the A28 passes through Birchington Station Road is on the left beside the church. It is pedestrianised, so it is best to park and then walk on foot to find Mulberrys Restaurant & Tea Rooms at 2 Station Road. They offer a range of light lunches as well as cakes and pastries in the afternoon, but close surprisingly early at 3.30pm on some days.

92

The city walls of Canterbury. The majority of what stands today is of medieval date, but these walls stand on Roman foundations and in places the distinctive Roman squared stone blocks bonded with thin bricks can be seen standing to a height of six feet or more within the later rebuilding.

The Church Route

Start: Royal Oak, Holt Street, Nonington,
Dover, CT15 4HT. Tel: 01304 841012

Finish: Peggoty's Tea Room, 122 High Street,
Tenterden, TN30 6HT. Tel: 01580 764393

The little village of Nonington lies east of the A2 and west of the A256 about ten miles northwest of Dover. The village is a straggling affair, so finding the Royal Oak without a satnav is a bit of a challenge. It is probably easiest to find the church first, then head south along the lane to a T-junction. The pub is off to your right.

Leaving the pub head south to follow the signs along some tortuous narrow lanes to Barfrestone. The beautiful little parish church lies at the southern end of the village. This is a real gem of

The Yew Tree pub at Barfrestone is one of the most welcoming village inns to be found in Kent.

The magnificently embellished South Door of Barfrestone church is a masterpiece of Norman stone carving. This quality of work is usually found only in cathedrals.

Norman work dating to about 1150 when the village formed part of the estates of the de Port family. Presumably it was the de Ports who paid for the magnificent carvings that make this such a spectacular church, but nobody is certain. The glory of the church is the main doorway, carved with a representation of Christ in Glory surrounded by numerous figures of knights, hunters, ladies, cooks, musicians and other everyday folk of the time. The carvings seem identical in style to some of about the same date at Rochester Cathedral and were presumably carved by the same artists.

Leave Barfrestone along lanes signposted at first to Barham and then to Adisham. You will pass through Elvington and Nonington to Ratling and Adisham. The church here is another Norman construction. It lacks the rich ornamentation found at Barfrestone, but does have a sturdy tower topped by a highly unusual pyramid roof. The church also boasts some fine windows of 13th century date. Note that Church Lane is a very narrow cul-de-sac with nowhere to park your car. You should park on the village green and then walk to the church.

From Adisham head north again to Bekesbourne, then bear left to Patrixbourne. This is the third church within this small area to boast fine Norman work. The doorway here is similar to that at Barfrestone in that its main feature is a carving of Christ. The rest of the ornamentation is not as richly finished as at Barfrestone, but it is worth a look nonetheless.

Leave Patrixbourne along the lane towards Canterbury. Join the city ring road and leave the city heading southwest on the A28 towards Ashford and Hastings. At Bagham bear right onto the A252 to Maidstone. After less than a mile turn left down a lane to Chilham. Parking here is limited due to the

The enigmatic "grinning monster" carving that features on the North Door of Barfrestone church.

narrow streets, but there is a car park on the edge of the village that is only a short walk to the church.

95

The parish church at Chilham is younger than those visited so far, dating mostly to the 15th century. It is a masterpiece of Perpendicular Gothic on a small scale that well repays taking the time to have a good look round. The rest of the village is likewise worth strolling around. The old village square is lined by Tudor and Jacobean houses and has not changed much in four centuries.

Return to the A28 and continue southwest towards Ashford. Just before entering Ashford turn left at a roundabout to join the A2070. Follow this road across the junction with the M20, then turn left along the A20 towards Folkestone. After only a mile turn right down the

The wonderful fruit cake on offer at Peggoty's tea room in Tenterdon. There is a constantly changing range of tasty cakes on offer at this charming little tea shop.

The church at Adisham features some fine Norman stonework, though it was remodelled in medieval times.

lane that leads to **Mersham.** This is another Norman church, though one that has been much enlarged and altered over the centuries. The main interest here lies in the large number of splendid tombs, particularly the 1765 tomb of Sir Wyndham Knatchbull by William Tyler.

Leave Mersham, returning to the A20. Turn left back towards Ashford. At a roundabout turn left on to the A2070 towards Rye. At Hamstreet turn right on to the B2067 to Tenterden. This lovely little town is dominated by its church. The church tower rises to an impressive 100 feet and is often open to the public. Locals will tell you that on a very clear day, and if you have a good telescope, you can see the French coast. Reputedly this is the furthest inland that this feat is possible. The church is one of only five in the country to have twin west doors.

One of the bizarre monsters that were carved on to the church at Patrixbourne almost a thousand years ago. Despite having suffered some weathering over the centuries, the carvings remain real attractions.

Having visited the church turn east along the High Street, the A28, to find Peggoty's Tea Room. The helpful staff here will be only too delighted to show you the wide range of homemade cakes that are baked fresh daily and feature a constantly changing range of recipes. When I called I had the fruit cake - it was one of the finest I have ever tasted. They are open 10am to 5pm Monday to Saturday and 11am to 5pm on Sundays.

97

The church at Mersham retains its solid Norman tower, though the body of the church has been much enlarged and altered over the centuries.

A boat lies forlornly high and dry at low tide at Otterham Quay.

The Oyster Coast

Start: Green Lion, 104 High Street,
Rainham, ME8 8AD. Tel: 01634 377200

Finish: The Tea & Times, 36a, High Street,
Whitstable, Kent CT5 1BQ. Tel: 01227 262639

The north Kent coast is famous for its wildlife and its seafood, which attract visitors in equal numbers. This drive winds its way along the coastline taking in a variety of views and villages.

You will find the Green Lion easily enough in Rainham High Street. Leave the pub and take the B2004 off the A2 towards the eastern end of Rainham. Where the B2004 turns sharp left, turn right along a lane to Otterham Quay and find the pub on a roundabout. The waters to the north of the pub form the tidal estuary of the Medway River. There are numerous islands among the mud flats and tidal sandbanks, most of which are owned by the Royal Society for the Protection of Birds which maintain them as wildlife refuges. Although so close to London and even more so to the Medway Towns, this little village manages to have an atmosphere of utter wildness and isolation. The Otterham Creek is tidal and muddy. Continue through the little village to reach Upchurch and then Lower Halstow.

The village of Lower Halstow stands on a low hill amid pasture land. In previous centuries this was an island among the marshes and winding tidal waterways. There is a small harbour here that is mostly occupied by yachts and pleasure craft. Traces of a Roman settlement have been found here. It is thought that the Roman era settlement was a fishing village. Certainly large numbers of oyster shells have been found here.

The oyster is now a food linked to luxury and wealth, but it was not always so. Until pollution from industrial cities began to pollute coastal waters in the 19th and 20th centuries, oysters were astonishingly common along shorelines such as that of north Kent. Indeed, the oyster

The peculiar running man sign that stands outside the churchyard at Upchurch. The figure's arms and legs are jointed and can be moved into different positions.

was traditionally a food of the poor and was especially linked to the East End of London. Vast quantities of oysters from Kent and Essex were taken to London to feed the East End. As late as World War I, oysters were recommended as an invalid food being easily digested and nutritious. They were fed most often to men who had suffered abdominal wounds and so could not digest other foods. Oysters are found in the mud to this day, but eating them is not recommended unless the purity of the water can be assured.

In Victorian times the Kentish oysters were collected by boats dragging a net with an iron scraper at its mouth. The net had a mesh large enough to catch only those oysters aged about 18 months or more. These were collected and taken to artificial pits dug along the shoreline where they were stored for several weeks. The sea water was allowed to flow in and out of the pits at high tide in carefully controlled amounts. The aim was to produce a semi-stagnant water which would impart a green colour to the oysters and so increase their market value.

Maintaining the Kent oysterbeds was taken very seriously. Large areas of oysterbeds were fished only in the month of May, being left for the rest of the year to allow the oysters living there to breed successfully and so restock the areas that were fished. It was illegal to take a young oyster, the official measure being that any oyster between the shells of which, when closed, a shilling would rattle was too small. Punishments were severe.

From Lower Halstow head northeast along the lane to Iwade. The marshes to your left along this lane hide a grim past. Hidden amid the tidal creeks is the ominously named Deadman's Island. After the Great Plague of 1665 any ship heading for London was stopped and searched for a person showing signs of illness. Any person who was found suffering from a symptom that might be plague was put into one of several ships anchored in the mouth of the Medway as quarantine vessels. Those unfortunates who died were buried in unmarked graves on Deadman's Island. How many bodies lie there is quite unknown, but certainly runs into hundreds.

At Iwade turn left along the A249 and cross Kingsferry Bridge onto the Isle of Sheppey. About half a mile beyond the bridge turn right down a lane to the Elmley Marshes Reserve run by the

101

The bleak landscape of Graveney Marshes, now preserved for posterity as a nature reserve.

Royal Society for Protection of Birds. This reserve stretches for more than two miles along the coast of Sheppey and embraces 3,300 acres of marsh and mudflats favoured by wading birds. It is estimated that some 10,000 wigeon, 4,000 teal and 2,000 white-fronted geese overwinter here each year. Breeding birds include redshank, lapwings and shovelers. The hides at Kings Hill offer fine views and are open most days of the year.

Return over the bridge and follow the B2005 into Sittingbourne. Leave Sittingbourne on the A2 heading east. Just beyond Faversham turn left along a lane to Goodnestone and Graveney. Beyond Graveney the lane pushes out across Graveney Marshes to reach the coast at the isolated Sportsman Inn. This area is another nature reserve, the South Swale Local Nature Reserve which is run by the Kent Trust for Nature Conservation. As at Elmley it is wading birds that are most attracted to this site. Brent Geese are especially numerous.

102

At the Sportsman Inn follow the lane as it bends east to follow the coast to Seasalter. Beyond Seasalter the road enters Whitstable, once a leading seaside resort for Londoners. The town dates back to Roman times and remained a thriving fishing centre until the 1950s. Even today the town is famed for its oysters, and there are numerous seafood eateries where they can be enjoyed. The shingle beach is lined by black-tarred fishermen's sheds and by small fishermen's cottages.

Boats pulled up on to the beach at Whitstable Harbour.

For 'foodies' the main reason to visit is the annual Oyster Festival. This is held each summer, centring around 25 July. This is the day dedicated to St James, the patron saint of oysters. The symbolic heart of the Festival is the 'Landing of the Oysters', when Whitstable Sea Scouts bring oysters ashore for a formal blessing by clergy before they are presented to the Lord Mayor. They are then passed to inns and restaurants as part of the vibrant Oyster Parade as it travels through the town centre.

The Blessing of the Waters service is still held at Reeves Beach on one of the Festival evenings, today organised by the Association of Men of Kent and Kentish Men, and the local tradition of Grotter building (creating hollow mounds of sand or mud with an outside decoration of oyster shells) is still practised on the same day. Originally built by children who would beg "a penny for the grotter" much as other children did for Guy Fawkes, today's grotters are built purely for the fun of it and lit by candles to produce an intriguing night-time spectacle.

103

Whether you visit during the Festival or not you should try to buy some local seafood to take home to enjoy. More immediately, find the Tea & Times tearooms at 36a High Street. The cafe is open seven days a week, and serves roast lunches on a Sunday.

Fishing sheds at Whitstable Harbour. The fish and other seafood caught by the boats operating out of Whitstable is sold at a small market beside these huts.

Charing church and adjacent buildings that were once ecclesiastical in nature but have now been converted into houses.

The Stour Valley

Start: The White Horse, Lenham Heath Road, Sandway, Maidstone, Kent ME17 2HY. Tel: 01622 859511

Finish: Pav's Tea Gardens, 1, St. Mildred's Gardens, Westgate-on-Sea, Kent CT8 8TP. Tel: 01843 831851

The Stour is the second largest river in Kent, draining most of the east of the county. In fact this is not one river, but three rivers that join to flow into the sea together near Sandwich. This drive follows the longest of the three rivers, the Great Stour. The Little Stour is about 9 miles long and the East Stour 10 miles long.

The drive starts just outside Lenham, named for the River Len which also rises nearby but which flows west to be a tributary of the Medway. **Find the White Horse by leaving the A20 at Lenham and heading south out of the village on the lane to Leadingcross Green and Boughton Malherbe.** The pub stands on the Sandway crossroads just after the lane crosses a railway and before it crosses the M20.

Leaving the pub drive north to the A20, then turn right towards Ashford. Just after the junction with the A252 the village of Charing will be to your left. Enter the village to find the church. This charming place appears to be more of a small town than a village. The ruins of what was once a palace owned by the Archbishops of Canterbury lie just outside and are worth a visit.

Return to the A20 and continue into Ashford. This was a relatively unimportant village until the railway was built through here in the 19th century. It was chosen to be a major repair and maintenance centre for the railways, and the little village grew rapidly to become a town. The East Stour flows into the Great Stour just south of Ashford. **At Ashford turn northeast along the A28 towards Canterbury.**

About three miles outside Ashford turn right along a lane leading

The large sundial on the village green at Charing. The metal plate is marked with dates. To make the sundial work visitors need to stand with their toes on the correct date, when their shadow will tell the correct time on the surrounding dial.

to Wye. This village has houses that date mostly to the Georgian period. For some reason the local builders chose to include grotesque heads and figures on many of the houses. It is a pleasant enough place, and the church is worth a look, but the real attraction lies along the lane east of the village to Hastingleigh. The hill above the lane is dominated by a huge white crown about 180 feet tall. The hill figure was formed by hacking through the green turf to reveal the white chalk underneath.

The Wye Crown was first cut in 1902 by students from Wye Agricultural College working under the guidance of the Vice Principal T.J. Young. Young copied a drawing of a crown from a florin (a coin worth two shillings) and stuck it on his theodolite. He then got students carrying flags to climb the hill and peered through his theodolite so that he could direct them to place the flags so that they marked out the shape of the crown. Once the flags were in place, the students turned out en masse and completed the cutting of the figure in just four days.

The figure was cut to celebrate the coronation of King Edward VII. On the night of the coronation the crown was illuminated by 1500 fairy lamps, a feat repeated in 1935 for the silver jubilee of Edward's son King George V. During World War II the Wye Crown was covered up by having heaps of brushwood piled over it. The move was prompted by the fear that German bomber pilots would use the hill figure as an aid to navigation: it would certainly stand out clearly when seen from the air on moonlit nights. The Wye Crown is kept in good condition by the current students.

Having viewed the Wye Crown, return to Wye and turn right along the lane to Godmersham. At the junction with the A28 turn right towards Canterbury. The city of Canterbury is by far the largest settlement along the Stour. Despite the best efforts of those who covered up the Wye Crown, the bomber pilots of the Luftwaffe found the city easily enough. In 1940 and 1941 the German bombs destroyed a third of the ancient city centre. Fortunately they missed the Cathedral and most other historic buildings. This drive bypasses the city centre,

107

The Wye Crown dominates the lane east of the village that leads towards Hastingleigh.

108

The fine sculpture of an RAF fighter pilot that stands outside the Manston Museum. Inside the museum are a preserved Spitfire and Hurricane together with a vast wealth of other objects dating back to the Battle of Britain in 1940.

but if you want to stop to explore feel free to do so. Just remember to keep an eye on the time so that you do not arrive at the drive's end too late for afternoon tea.

Leave Canterbury heading northwest along the A28 towards Margate. This road follows the course of the lower Stour, with the river rarely being more than 200 yards to the right of the road. **At Sarre bear right along the A253, then turn right on the A299 at Monkton. At Monkton turn left at a roundabout on to the B2190 and follow this road to Kent International Airport.** This was formerly the RAF fighter base of Manston, which saw much action during World War II. There is a museum here that houses a Spitfire and a Hurricane as well as a vast range of other exhibits. It is well worth a visit.

After viewing the museum at Manston, head north along the B2048 across the Isle of Thanet leaving the mouth of the Stour a mile to the south. Follow the B2048 into Westgate. This was formerly a separate village, but in late Victorian and Edwardian times it was massively developed to become a suburb of Margate, to the east.

A Spitfire Mk1 of the type that flew from RAF Manston to battle the German Luftwaffe during the dramatic days of the Battle of Britain in 1940.

There are two fine beaches here where you might be tempted to go paddling on hot summer's days, or at least to buy an ice cream. On a hill at the eastern end of the village is a lovely sunken garden that is worth a visit.

Pav's Tea Gardens overlooks St Mildred's Bay, just west of the car park and slipway on Royal Esplanade. In truth this is more of a beach cafe than a conventional teashop, but it does serve some nice cakes and the views are simply stunning. Pav's is open 8am to 4pm in the winter months and 8am to 7pm in the summer, staying open longer on sunny weekends if business is brisk.

The White Horse offers both traditional British and authentic Mexican Cuisine in the heart of the Kent countryside. This beautiful *The White Horse*

300-year-old building offers a blend of antiquated features fused with a comfortable and modern decor. A family-run pub with a great family-orientated atmosphere, there is both an indoor and outdoor childrens' play area. Real ales and a selection of fine lagers served. Open Monday - Friday 5.00pm - 11.00pm. Saturday 12.00 noon - midnight. Sunday 12.00 noon - 10.30pm. www.the-white-horse.com

110

The fine view from the verandah outside Pav's Tea Gardens at Westgate-on-Sea.